EDUCATING OUTSIDE

EDUCATING OUTSIDE

BY HELEN PORTER

B L O O M S B U R Y

LONDON · OXFORD · NEW YORK · NEW DELHI · SYDNEY

Bloomsbury Education
An imprint of Bloomsbury Publishing Plc

50 Bedford Square	1385 Broadway
London	New York
WC1B 3DP	NY 10018
UK	USA

www.bloomsbury.com

First published in Great Britain 2018

Quotes from the National Curriculum documents used in this publication are approved under an Open Government Licence: http://www.nationalarchives.gov.uk/doc/open-government-licence/version/3/

Every reasonable effort has been made to trace copyright holders of material reproduced in this book, but if any have been inadvertently overlooked the publishers would be glad to hear from them.

For legal purposes the Acknowledgements on p. viii constitute an extension of this copyright page.

A catalogue record for this book is available from the British Library.

Library of Congress Cataloguing-in-Publication data has been applied for.

ISBN
PB: 978-1-4729-4629-4
ePub: 978-1-4729-4628-7
ePDF: 978-1-4729-4630-0

4 6 8 10 9 7 5 3

Typeset by Newgen KnowledgeWorks Pvt. Ltd., Chennai, India
Printed and bound in India by Replika Press Pvt. Ltd.

This book is produced using paper that is made from wood grown in managed, sustainable forests. It is natural, renewable and recyclable. The logging and manufacturing processes conform to the environmental regulations of the country of origin.

To find out more about our authors and books visit www.bloomsbury.com. Here you will find extracts, author interviews, details of forthcoming events and the option to sign up for our newsletters.

Contents

Acknowledgements   viii
Foreword   ix

Introduction   1
    Why this book?   1
    Why outdoor learning?   1
    Who is this book for?   4
    Subjects included   5
    Resources   5
    Tips for getting started   6
    All systems go!   8
    Final reflections   9

1. Outdoor Learning in Practice   10
    The setting   10
    The conception of an idea   10
    Early days of planning   11
    The day to day experiences   12
    Moving forward   12
    Next steps   14
    Lessons to be learned   14

2. Science Outdoors   16
    What does the National Curriculum say?   16
    Working scientifically   17
    Plants: Year 1   18
    Plants: Year 2   20
    Plants: Year 3   22
    Animals, including humans: Year 1   26
    Animals, including humans: Year 2   28
    Animals, including humans: Year 3   29
    Animals, including humans: Year 4   30
    Animals, including humans: Year 6   32
    Animals, including humans investigations   34
    Materials: Year 1   35

Materials: Year 2   36
Materials investigations   36
States of matter: Year 4   37
Rocks: Year 3   38
Seasonal change: Year 1   40
Living things and their habitats: Year 2   41
Living things and their habitats: Year 4   44
Living things and their habitats: Year 5   46
Living things and their habitats: Year 6   47
Living things and their habitats investigations   48
Light: Year 3   48
Light: Year 6   49
Light investigations   50
Sound: Year 4   50
Sound investigations   51
Earth and space: Year 5   52
Earth and space investigation   53
Evolution and inheritance: Year 6   53
Evolution and inheritance investigation   53

3. History Outdoors   54
    What does the National Curriculum say?   54
    Key stage 1   57
    Key stage 2   60
    Changes in Britain from the Stone Age to the Iron Age: Key stage 2   60
    The Roman Empire and its impact on Britain: Key stage 2   64
    The Anglo-Saxons, Scots and Vikings: Key stage 2   69
    The achievements of the earliest civilizations: Key stage 2   73
    Ancient Greece: Key stage 2   76
    Non-European city: Key stage 2   80

4. Geography Outdoors   83
    What does the National Curriculum say?   83
    Locational knowledge: Key stage 1 and 2   83
    Place knowledge: Key stage 1   87
    Place knowledge: Key stage 2   90
    Human and physical geography: Key stage 1   90
    Human and physical geography: Key stage 2   91
    Geographical skills and fieldwork: Key stage 1   96
    Geographical skills and fieldwork: Key stage 2   97

5. Art and Design Outdoors   100
    What does the National Curriculum say?   100
    Using materials found outside   101
    Using the outside as stimulus   103
    Big art inspired by artists   105

6. English Outdoors   107
    What does the National Curriculum say?   107
    Reading   108
    Writing   110
    Spelling   112
    Grammar   112

7. Maths Outdoors   114
    What does the National Curriculum say?   114
    Number   115
    Measurement   117
    Geometry   118
    Statistics (Year 3 and Year 6)   119
    Ratio and proportion (Year 6)   120
    Algebra (Year 6)   120

Final thoughts   121

Bibliography and useful links   122
Index   123

Acknowledgements

Even though this is my first book, I am going to make the assumption that books are rarely written in isolation. This one certainly wouldn't have seen the light of day if it wasn't for a number of key people.

Jenny Jones, the Headteacher at Anstey Junior School, had the faith in me to give me such a fantastic job that allowed the development of these ideas. Sam Campbell, my teaching assistant, is a constant source of support and encouragement, without whom many of the ideas in this book could never have happened. The other staff, children and parents at Anstey (past and present) have also been encouraging, exciting and supportive – thank you all.

Other schools have joined us on this journey. I have worked with St Michael's in Aldershot, Vernon Terrace Primary in Northampton, Sheet Primary and Froxfield Primary in Hampshire. I shared ideas at the South Downs National Park Teacher's conference, and have run courses for teachers. I have also worked with the staff and students at Winchester University. Barry Harwood and Matt Prince in particular have supported, encouraged and provided opportunities for me to develop and hopefully inspire future teachers. Thank you to all who have shared the enthusiasm for outdoor learning.

Thanks also to Peter Holt and Rob Crook. Peter has not only proofread this book, but has accompanied every reply with words of praise and encouragement that have kept me on track to meet the deadline I was working towards. Rob provided me with his technical skills and experience so that the website www.outsidelearning.co.uk could be developed as an initial platform for some of the ideas contained in this book.

And finally, thanks to my family: my parents for their support not only with this venture, but also with my MA; my husband, Jon, for indulging me with the time to make this happen; and my children, James and Gemma – little did I know that hours in the car waiting while they were training for triathlons or cricket could have been so useful!

Foreword

Educating Outside provides teachers and student teachers that are new to the idea of outdoor learning with an excellent springboard from which to develop their practice in teaching curricular subjects outside the classroom. Helen Porter has tried, tested and evaluated the success of the lesson plans contained within the book in a real primary school context and most importantly, they have ringing endorsement from the pupils and the support of the senior leadership team.

This book builds upon strong research evidence about multiple benefits for children of learning outside the classroom in natural environments. Recently, this research has been drawn together in three reports which are freely accessible online. There is ample evidence that taking teaching outside can transform children's enjoyment and engagement with learning, raising levels of concentration, persistence and understanding. Helen's book recognises that supporting all children's attainment is paramount for schools and her focus on National Curriculum links enables teachers to provide access to outdoor learning's wider benefits, whilst still meeting and indeed enhancing curriculum learning objectives. It does not demand *extra* time for outdoor learning but instead encourages teachers to use curriculum time differently. This chimes precisely with the findings of the Natural Connections project, which found that schools used outdoor learning to boost pupil experience and learning across all curriculum subjects, embedding these opportunities within whole school practice.

One of the key things that Helen has recognised, however, is that starting out doing something differently can require a substantial initial investment of time. To provide a springboard for change, she has compiled a set of lesson plans within topics, with a specific curriculum learning objective, cross-curricular links and soft skills development. There are also details of resources and what to do across year groups for Science, History and Geography, with guidance about other ideas for Art and Design, English and Maths. These practical plans offer the sort of inspiration that can be subsequently adapted and shaped according to local situations, but they will avoid constant re-inventing of the wheel in terms of making links to learning objectives. This book will help to overcome the two most common barriers reported in Natural Connections, making links to the curriculum and teacher confidence.

One of the most valuable aspects of *Educating Outside* within current literature on outdoor play and learning is that it puts *education* squarely first rather than listing fun outdoor activities to try. Helen started her development of outdoor learning at Anstey Junior School by looking at medium term plans and identifying opportunities to take some teaching outside. Her aim is that every class teacher at Anstey Junior School includes lessons outside as part of their repertoire of teaching.

Embedded and sustainable outdoor learning has the potential to change teachers' and children's lives for the better (see link to Transforming Outdoor Learning in Schools (see page viii)); I warmly recommend *Educating Outside* to primary schools beginning to make that change.

Sue Waite, Reader Emeritus, Plymouth University

Introduction

Why this book?

When I started as the 'outdoor teacher' at Anstey Junior School, my brief was to engage the children in exciting, stimulating and purposeful learning in the school grounds. The main short term aims of my job were to plan enriching learning opportunities that were linked to the curriculum, whilst helping the children to develop their levels of concentration and resilience through outdoor experiences. There was also the aim of equalising the opportunities for all the children in the school, allowing them all to benefit from practical hands-on experiences which would inspire them, in addition to helping them develop a better understanding of the curriculum areas we investigated together.

So, armed with the medium term planning from each year group, I started to look for curriculum-linked outdoor learning ideas. I searched the web but came up with very little. There are ideas for the Early Years Foundation Stage (EYFS) and some for key stage 1. There is also a lot of support for the Forest School approach and creative activities – but I couldn't find much about how to teach elements of history, geography or even science outside. So although there was enthusiasm within my school for what I was being asked to do, and when I spoke to teacher friends they were supportive of and interested in my new role, I couldn't easily find resources to support my planning.

This then started to link directly with research I was carrying out for my dissertation. In broad terms, research shows that:

- teachers understand the benefits of outdoor learning
- the vast majority of teachers believe they should use their schools grounds more for learning
- outdoor learning declines as children go through the primary phase
- teachers feel under time pressures to 'fit everything in'
- risk assessments and cost can be a barrier to trips
- there is a lack of ideas for Learning Outside the Classroom (LOtC) linked to the curriculum.

So, this book is hopefully part of the answer: a bank of curriculum-linked outdoor learning ideas, which can be carried out in the school grounds with minimal (if any) expense, need no additional risk assessments and are curriculum-linked so require no extra time in the day… Bingo!

Why outdoor learning?

Outdoor learning is fun. It is also engaging, messy, collaborative and creative. But, from a more serious perspective, if we put outdoor learning into the context of the world children are growing up in today, its importance increases:

- The number of children who are classed as overweight or obese in our country is rising.
- The number of children and young adults in this country who have mental health problems is increasing.

- The level of physical activity and the amount of time children spend outside is decreasing.
- The range of experiences children have now is reducing – it is said that about 50% of primary school children haven't made a sandcastle on the beach. I have worked with children who have never seen a bonfire, or been to their local museum (which is free to enter), or been for a walk in the woods.
- The number of children who are NEETs (Neither in Education, Employment nor Training), or who are at risk of becoming a NEET is concerning.

The reasons for these statistics are varied and complex, but spending time outside can have a positive influence on all of them. Research suggests that outdoor learning has a wealth of positive impacts. Outdoor learning:

- increases confidence and self-esteem;
- improves emotional health and wellbeing;
- impacts positively on behaviour;
- increases attention and concentration;
- increases motivation and resilience;
- increases pupil engagement in their learning;
- adds depth to the curriculum;
- is inspiring and motivating, providing memorable experiences;
- provides opportunities for cross-curricular links;
- links to improved attendance;
- improves achievement and progress.

And I would certainly add to this list, having heard a child who said it is impossible to learn outside because there isn't an interactive whiteboard out there, that going outside to learn helps children to understand that learning is an on-going, continual process. Learning shouldn't be confined to books and classrooms – it can and does happen anywhere, constantly. And if we want our children to be life-long learners, which is a desirable skill and mind set, then we have to enable them to see the possibilities of learning always and everywhere. Taking children outside to learn ought to be a part of this process.

It is also really interesting, and I think crucial, to see children working in a different environment. Children who can be reluctant, clumsy, or shy inside can shine when they are in a different location. They can become leaders, making wise decisions; they can be willing to try and fail and try again, whereas in the classroom, failure might stop them in their tracks. Children who struggle to get started in the classroom, can, when outside, be the first to see the way into a task. The ones who get distracted easily inside, or who have a whole list of work avoidance tactics up their sleeve, can often be the ones who stay on task for a whole session outside – and then complain that the time has gone too quickly!

Seeing children working in a different and usually more positive way outside can have huge knock-on effects back in the classroom. The children hold themselves in higher esteem because they have been learning in an environment that has allowed them to have success. The other children can also react differently to their peers. Some children, who struggle in the classroom, can be mothered by their peers, ignored, or even put down. Once these children shine outside, the perception the other children have can change dramatically. As such, successes outside can easily lead to more confidence and success back in the classroom, giving rise to positive benefits both for the individuals and the class as a whole.

It is also worth considering, at this stage, what skills the World Economic Forum (WEF) consider to be essential for today's children who will be joining the workforce within the next 20 years. The foundational literacies listed by the WEF include maths, science, literacy and ICT and are covered by the National Curriculum. However, if we move onto their essential competencies and character qualities, we can see where outdoor learning becomes really important. Included here are critical thinking, problem solving, communication, collaboration, creativity, curiosity, persistence, grit, initiative, leadership and adaptability.

If we are not only working with and celebrating the children we have in our classes at the moment, but also helping them to be ready for the next stages in their education and the life that will follow, we have a duty to consider how we support the development of character qualities and competencies. This is to ensure that they are fit and ready for both the present and the future. I would suggest that outdoor learning can play an important role in developing these areas. Working with other children outside allows them to take the lead, resolve differences of opinions, show resilience and develop creative approaches to a greater extent than may be possible in the classroom. I have seen children develop these skills, and exploit the opportunities to the full when working on challenges in the school grounds. They risk assess themselves, organise their time and resources and ask questions of each other, learning to give advice kindly and not to take it as a criticism! For some, this happens naturally and the skills and aptitudes are clear to see, but for others there is a need to be explicit, to give examples and support. Some of these skills do have to be modelled. Some children need to be shown, for example, how to give feedback in a supportive manner, or how to assume leadership roles. These ways of working may not happen overnight, especially if the children haven't experienced much learning other than in the classroom before. However, I do think we have a responsibility to help children grow and develop these competences and character qualities in a range of environments. There is no guarantee of immediate success – but it is worth persevering as the benefits will come.

I would also add that it has been suggested that when children play outside they use five times more words than they do when playing inside. When we are working with a generation of children for whom technology plays a huge part in their lives, I think we have a duty to give them opportunities to communicate and work face-to-face rather than in a virtual world, and outdoor learning does that too. A lot of the ideas suggested in this book will not work if the children are not able to communicate effectively. This means talking, listening and responding to what has been said. Some children will need support and scaffolding to enable them to be successful but, for many, having the opportunity will be enough. If there is specific vocabulary you would like the children to use when working outside, then do take lists out with you and practice them with the children. Do also, if necessary, model how to make suggestions. Teach the children that if their idea isn't chosen then that's OK (it doesn't mean it was a bad idea, just that someone else's is going to be tried first), and also how to behave appropriately if yours is chosen. Perhaps work through a scenario where elements of different people's ideas are combined. As suggested, some children will have the communication skills and the maturity required to manage this side of working outside, but for those who don't, we have to teach them. We can only do this by providing the opportunities, not avoiding them. At the end of sessions outside, celebrate the successes (especially those that may have come from adversity) and note who needs what support for next time.

The benefits of outdoor learning, I think, are well researched and widely accepted and I have begun, in a very small way, to demonstrate how the research ties in with elements of practice, although this will be greatly developed in other areas of this book. It is worth underling now though that research suggests that nearly 80% of teachers feel that their schools underuse their outside spaces. This means that although the evidence is strong, work still needs to be done to support teachers taking their classes outside to work. Hopefully this book will help.

Brain function and physical activity

There is an increasing body of evidence that links physical activity and mental activity. Recent studies have shown that memory is improved by doing something physical in the hours after revising. I show the children I work with scanned images of the brain that highlight levels of activity after someone has been sitting quietly for 20 minutes, and after someone has been engaged in 20 minutes of physical activity. The differences are striking. It is for these reasons, among others, that I take children out to do quizzes, information searches and alike. I am explicit with them about the fact that physical activity enhances brain activity and that their learning should be enhanced by the approach we are using. So, although it is clear that some of the learning opportunities described in this book could take place in the classroom, I believe there is compelling evidence to support transferring them to the outside.

Who is this book for?

If you are a teacher or a student teacher who wishes to enrich and enhance the experiences of children in your class by taking learning beyond the classroom, this book is for you. It is written for all of you in education who can be persuaded of the benefits of LOtC, in terms of children's wellbeing, emotional, social and academic development. It is written for all of you who are willing to recognise that learning happens all the time, in different locations, with different outcomes, and that these wider experiences can have a positive, sometimes magical impact, on more traditional learning. It is written for all teachers who recognise that not all children thrive within the classroom environment and that, by taking children to work outside, we are encouraging the development of a range of skills that can have a positive impact on all learning. This book is for teachers who understand that not all children bring a wealth of experience with them to school and that practical learning can engage and broaden experiences. This book is written for all teachers who wish to extend and develop their practice in the best interests of their children, but who may need a few ideas to help them get started. In essence, and in my experience of working within the teaching profession for 20 years, this book is written for all teachers!

The ideas in this book have been developed as a direct result of my work with children in the outdoors, mostly in school but also in a field studies centre. The ideas are all linked to the National Curriculum programmes of study and can take place in the school grounds, meaning they are integral to what has to be taught and can be carried out within minutes of your classroom. The philosophy behind these ideas is based on my studies and current research in the field of outdoor learning. Most plans provide cross-curricular opportunities, resource lists, links to soft skills and suggested outcomes. The ideas are designed to support and extend your existing planning rather than replace it, so as to allow time for outside learning opportunities within your daily teaching and learning. This allows it to become integrated into your curriculum and the children's experiences. The ideas are also mostly to be seen as a starting point, not a final product, to be adapted and improved to suit you, your class and your setting.

I would also say that this book is for both individual teachers and for schools as a whole. There are obviously huge benefits in developing a whole-school approach to outdoor learning. A focus on this area can lead to ideas being shared amongst staff, children talking to each other about experiences, grants can be accessed for school grounds development and resources can be acquired. However, if your school has other priorities and the timing isn't right for a whole-school approach, then there should be nothing stopping the individual teacher from using the ideas in this book with his or her own class. As the suggestions in this book are linked to the curriculum, all you will be doing by adopting some of them is changing where the learning is taking place. You will know if you need to talk to anyone else in your school about giving these ideas a go, but hopefully, if you are keen, I have provided enough research to back up your enthusiasm and it would be really disappointing if someone stood in your way.

I do hope this book is useful and that it provides you with the tools and the information necessary to make a start on an outdoor learning adventure with your class. I hope you and your children enjoy the experiences and benefit from them.

Subjects included

I really believe that any subject can be taught outside. That doesn't mean that it has to happen all the time. It just means that, as teachers, we need to ask ourselves not only what are the children going to learn, but where is the best place to learn it. And there will be times when, for numerous reasons, the best place to learn will be somewhere other than the classroom.

The main body of this book is split into subject areas and relates directly to the requirements of the National Curriculum, as this is what we have to teach in maintained primary schools in the UK. I have concentrated my ideas on the areas of history, science, and geography. This is because not only do they provide fantastic outdoor learning opportunities in their own right, but they also allow for many cross-curricular opportunities that can be exploited. As such, although I have included sections on English and maths, they are relatively short and provide general ideas and themes that can be applied across different year groups, rather than detailed lesson ideas. I have also included a short section on art and design outside which will hopefully provide you with some ideas that can link into the work and topics you do.

The start of each chapter includes sections quoted from the Primary National Curriculum 2013, the full reference to which you can find in the Bibliography.

Resources

I do have to say that sometimes resourcing outdoor learning opportunities can take some time. Firstly, because you may not have done anything like this before and it is worth spending a bit of time to make sure you are happy. Secondly, it is worth making sure you are well organised, as depending on your school layout, it may not be that easy to go back in if you have forgotten something once outside. And thirdly, because it is worth laminating resources so you can use them again. The flip side is that, following a lesson outside, you probably won't have much marking to do and you may, as a result, have the resources, data, or information you need for a subsequent lesson. You should also find that one lesson outside leads to another, either inside or outside, and you can reuse the resources you have made. So perhaps the extra time needed to resource lessons outside isn't as much as it first appears.

For each curriculum idea in science, history, geography and art and design, I have listed the specific resources that are needed. However, there are a few general resources which I would recommend you having available:

- a camera: for evidence of work done, and to use as extension work back in class
- chalks: often useful for both you and the children
- clipboards: we don't always record, but there are times when it is useful to do so

We also managed to get a grant for wellies, but prior to this, I would inform children or parents and carers the day before they were needed so that children could bring some in from home. An alternative would be that, if going on the grass in winter, the children change into PE shoes to reduce the amount of mud brought back into school.

When using quiz or information cards, I would recommend laminating them if possible so they can be used over and over again, saving precious time. This is also true for pictures that you wish to take outside as inspiration for artwork, or recording charts that can then be written on with whiteboard pens and re-used. Also, if you make PowerPoints or similar for use in the classroom before you go outside, do save them in a logical place so they can be used again. I know from my own experiences how annoying it is when I have made a resource and then not filed it properly so had to start again.

I have gradually gathered and acquired other resources, from soft toys of woodland creatures to collections of rocks and, if you can find a storage space, I would recommend you doing so too! We have a storage 'box' outside for all our resources, including pencils, pens, rubbers, etc. that is available to all teachers, thus reducing the amount that needs to be carried outside.

We also are lucky enough to have a garden shed so resources that can get wet and/or muddy can be stored separately from others.

Tips for getting started

You are the expert on your class, their dynamics, abilities and the ways they work. However, the following suggestions may help take the first steps with the logistical side of outside learning.

Resourcing

As with all lessons, it is really important to be organised and have a plan when taking children outside to learn. Make sure your resources are already either outside, or ready to take out with you – it's worth stating again that once you are outside it can be tricky to come back inside if you have forgotten something.

Grouping

I think it is crucial that children work with others when outside. It is only through working in groups that they can develop the skills of team work, negotiation, listening, co-operation and many more. Talk is fundamental to the success of working outside to help develop these soft skills, but also to support the children in concreting the activities into memorable learning experiences.

You will know if you need to put your children into groups yourself, but I do try to let the children group themselves. When working outside, children often choose to work with different partners than in the classroom and I don't like to prohibit this. I also try to keep group numbers flexible, saying to the children, for example, 'Today you need to work in groups of three or four'. These make getting into groups easier and quicker, and should mean that no-one gets left out. However, if you feel that you would like to group the children initially as that would work best for all of you, then do so. Also, don't be afraid of engineering some groups by asking a child to work with a specific person, if you know that it is in their best interests.

I also try, if possible, to have a no-blame culture in groups. Prior to working we often talk about the qualities needed for the group to work successfully. If this doesn't happen and issues can be addressed and sorted, then I work with the children to try to develop success and help them to move on. But if the dynamics just aren't right then a child can be moved from one group to another with no blame attached. I don't see this as avoiding a situation, just that sometimes a change can be a positive move. As the teacher, you may have to make decisions and manage these situations. However, the more the children work outside, the more successful the groupings tend to be and if moves are necessary, the children may suggest moving groups themselves, rather than you having to intervene.

Safety and risk

The first thing to say is that it is unlikely that you will need to carry out risk assessments, unless you are using tools, fire, animals or the pond (if you have one). They may already be in existence anyway, so would simply need personalising for your situation. In terms of any inherent risks linked to working outside, the more you do it, the better the children get at judging it. You are also giving children the skills to assess and analyse risk in different situations, which in the risk-averse society we live in, has got to be a positive. Having said that, there are things you can put in place to make both you and the children more confident about working in the school grounds, and most of these will stem from the rules you already have in place in your school. We have three rules: Be Safe, Be Kind, and Be Respectful. We do talk about what these mean in different situations outside. A good example is to not run in the woodlands as there are trip hazards so it's not safe. We consider respect when making decisions and working as groups. I am sure that your school rules can easily be a starting point for setting parameters when working outside, but if they are not, do feel free to adopt our three and see if they help.

Working outside is sometimes a bit confusing for children at the very beginning. They need to know the difference between what you are doing in class time and what happens at playtime when they have free choice. This is quite easy to achieve by making expectations clear at the beginning. Firstly, make it clear that the school rules apply when learning outside as well as inside. If it helps to have a laminated sheet of whatever behaviour chart you use to take out with you, then do so (but I don't think you'll need it for long!). Also, set the boundaries for where you want the children to work. Use physical features to limit how far they can go (no further than the bin, up to those trees…). Maybe, on your first couple of expeditions outside, work on the playground so the limits are really clear and indisputable.

Initially, it is worth making it clear that the children need to be able to see you as then you will be able to see all of the class too. For your own peace of mind, it is useful to see how the children react to being outside, and by always being able to see them, you can judge if the children are making sensible choices.

Also, I would recommend that for the first couple of activities, pick things for the children to do, so that you can stand back and watch for at least some of the lesson. You don't want to get so engrossed working with a group that you can't support the rest of the class in moderating their behaviour if necessary. The fact-finding activities (see the history section, but very applicable to other curriculum areas) are great for this because you can set them up so you know where the children will be: they have to come back to you to record information, but they work independently in their pairs or groups. Short maths activities or even sharing books can also work as initial activities – the children can get used to moving from inside to outside, have a few (but limited) resources and be active, but in a controlled way where outcomes are apparent for all.

Some of these points may be being overcautious, and knowing your own class, completely unnecessary, but do make sure you set the children and yourself up to succeed. Think about your own and the children's experiences of learning outside, and take the necessary steps, especially in the early stages, to make sure sessions will be as successful as possible.

A word about chalk

A number of the ideas in this book involve mark making with chalk on the playground and I have included these ideas for a number of reasons. I think they are important as, whatever the scope of your school's grounds, you will have some tarmacked outdoor space. These are ideas that every teacher can access, wherever they teach. Additionally, I believe that they all have an educational benefit, supporting learning of aspects of the curriculum. But, they also encourage collaboration between children: they necessitate talking in order to be successful; they allow children to work on a larger scale compared to working on paper; and they allow for physical movement. They leave a temporary record on the playground of what the children have done and this can have positive knock-on effects. For example, other children will look and see what has been created, some of the work (e.g. the mazes) may be used by other children at playtimes, maths work may be discussed, artwork critiqued, and other teachers may also be inspired to take their children out if there is evidence of what you have done.

I have never had a problem with the longevity of chalk on the playground. Having photographed what you have done for evidence (if necessary), it is possible to wash it off with a stiff brush and water, but I have never done this. It rains often enough in the UK for chalk to be washed away fairly frequently. And even if no rain is forecast, children running and walking over the chalk at playtime will soon rub most of it away so that the space is clear enough for you, or someone else, to start again.

Come rain or shine?

I know it is much easier to take children outside to learn when the weather is pleasant and the sun is shining. I also know, from plenty of experience, that some of the learning described in this book depends on dry weather – chalk and rain just doesn't work. However, I do think we need to be showing the children we teach that we can go outside in many different sorts of weather. I have been out with a class in heavy rain, trying to work out where all the water goes – you can't do that when the sun's out! The children loved it, and learnt loads, first-hand, about the water cycle. They also loved the fact that two ducks decided to walk across our playground while we were outside! It is obviously important that the children are suitably dressed to be outside in all weathers, and you have to manage your time carefully to make sure no-one gets really wet or really cold (including you). However, unless the weather is dangerous, give it a go and teach children lessons that will last them a lifetime.

All systems go!

The next step is to take the plunge. I would firstly advise you read the section entitled 'Outdoor Learning in Practice' to ensure you have an overview of what outdoor learning can look like for you as an individual, but also potentially from a whole school perspective. Then look at the sections of this book that relate to what you're doing in class this term or next term and decide where to start. If you are nervous, you could always begin with a quiet reading session. You could meet your class outside straight after lunch with their reading books in a box (collected before they go to lunch) and a few spares. Sit in the shade, do the register and read (it saves a lot more time than going in to register and collect books to go back out again). Or, you could go out for the last 10 minutes of the school day to read, with the children having collected their going home things. This could either be individual reading or a class story. It could be reading to each other, taking it in turns to read paragraphs; it could involve acting out or reading a play in small groups – so much easier outside than in the classroom! With more proficient readers, it could involve discussion of questions in a group… I worked with one school which was going to finish the day with a story outside, but invite parents to come and sit and join in as they arrived at school to pick their children up. If reading at home isn't embedded with some families within your school, this seems like a great way to get parents involved in reading to or with their children, or for you as a teacher to model to them how to read to their children.

Times tables hopscotch (see page 115) is also a good, short activity that is easily resourced and managed but very worthwhile. The trick is, at the start, to pick learning opportunities outside that you feel comfortable with. Build from there, knowing that the children will enjoy and benefit from what you do.

Once routines are established for working outside, all of the ideas in this book – and more – become possible. Good luck and enjoy!

Final reflections

As reflective practitioners, we will always think, in some way, about the work we do with children and I consider this to be especially important when trying out new ideas. Thoughts and reflections don't have to be a formal exercise, but can be if that's the way you work best. I do think it worthwhile to spend a little time thinking about: what worked well, what you would change; what the children learnt; how the learning outside supported what you were doing in the classroom; whether the children used or developed the necessary soft skills; how could you promote these further next time?; whether all necessary resources were available – the list is almost endless. But these reflections should be used as a way to move forward and improve next time, not to beat yourself up about what wasn't right! Celebrate the positives because there will be lots, and work with your children to develop some fantastic, memorable outside learning experiences.

1 Outdoor Learning in Practice

The introduction of outside learning is one of many initiatives that have been introduced at Anstey Junior School since the current Headteacher took over in 2012. In order to put the main content of this book into context, I think it is useful and important to investigate the reasons behind the development of outdoor learning in our setting, the process that the school has been through in order to get to our current situation and what we consider the next steps to be. It is important (and obvious) to state that this is just one school's journey and each school which introduces new initiatives will be unique, but I do believe there are lessons from our experience that can be learnt and applied to other settings. I hope, whilst reading this chapter, that you will be able to draw some parallels between Anstey Junior and your school, and between our children and the ones you teach. I hope you will be able to share in the journey we have taken, and use it as inspiration for how you might approach outdoor learning within your own context.

It is also important to underline here that although we are aiming for a whole-school approach to outside learning at Antsey, it is still within the power and realms of the individual teacher to introduce and develop outside learning with their own class – even if the school isn't yet ready to progress as a whole. The process of developing a whole-school approach is a long one and there are many ways to achieve it. But one option is for individual teachers to try out new ideas and make them work. This can then have a knock-on effect on other teachers and, over time, progress can be made as a whole-school. But even if you are the only teacher in the school who embraces outdoor learning, if you can see that it is making a positive difference to the children you teach, then you are doing the right thing!

The setting

Anstey Junior School is a two-form entry school in Alton and is situated in the most deprived ward in East Hampshire. We have a mixed catchment and intake, with around 25% of our children receiving Pupil Premium and approximately 35% on the SEN register. Since January 2012 the number of pupils on role has increased from just over 200 pupils to 252, meaning the school is at capacity in the majority of classes.

In addition to eight classrooms over two floors, we have a newly refurbished library, a hall, two working/meeting rooms, a couple of working areas outside the classrooms, and an outdoor space. This comprises of two tarmacked playground spaces; two fields, one of which is bordered by trees (only three deep); a small pond; four raised planting beds; and a potato plot. We are in the process of developing a fire lighting area that will hopefully include permanent tables for working, and we have a new storage shed and a welly store.

The conception of an idea

Jenny (the newly appointed Headteacher of Anstey) and I had worked together on and off for a number of years, in a couple of different schools since 1999. In 2012, when Jenny took on the headship, I was working part-time in another local school, part-time in a field studies centre and I was also studying for an MA (specialising in Outdoor Learning) at Winchester University. I started doing some supply work at Anstey, and Jenny and I had some conversations about whether we might be able to use some of my skills and knowledge to develop outdoor learning within the school. Jenny's thinking behind the conversations was multi-layered:

- If you talk to adults about their memories of school, most will recall either key teachers or trips and visits.
- Levels of concentration and resilience within many children in the school were lower than hoped, and outdoor learning is proven to support these soft skills.
- Outdoor learning can make the curriculum more exciting and engaging and this was seen to be important at this particular point in the school's development.
- Research suggests that many children are missing out on first-hand experiences now, and if we are expecting children to write creatively, problem solve and engage in their learning, we have to ensure they have concrete experiences.
- There are a myriad of other benefits of outdoor learning that would prove beneficial for the children and teachers within the school.

So, I was appointed to work two mornings a week, covering teacher's PPA time and teaching each class once a fortnight. The brief was to teach beyond the classroom (unless the weather meant it was dangerous to do so), and learning experiences had to be linked to the curriculum that term.

Why curriculum-linked outdoor learning and not something along the lines of the Forest School approach? Because time is precious in primary schools, and the easiest way to sell the idea of outdoor learning to staff members is to show that what is being taken outside is learning that has to be done anyway. All we are doing is thinking about the best place to learn, and finding opportunities for this to be outside. The question I always pose when considering what to take outside is 'where is the best place to learn?'. For example, when studying habitats, would the children benefit more from going outside and seeing and experiencing for real, or looking at textbooks or doing research on the internet? Although there is a time and a place for work inside, I am of the opinion that taking children outside gives them the first-hand experiences many are missing. It allows them to work in different, more active and practical ways where brain activity can be enhanced by physical activity and fresh air. The type of learning that takes place is more relevant and memorable, potentially leading to deeper learning experiences.

So my initial challenges were to put the theory into practice and develop some quality learning experiences linked to the curriculum, which would be based outside, supporting the children and the school in the areas agreed and outlined above.

But there was a secondary, more challenging element to what I was being asked to do. As the evidence for outdoor learning is compelling, Jenny asked me to not only work with the children, but also with the staff to develop a whole-school strategy and approach. I needed to consider how outdoor learning could be developed so that it became an integral and regular part of the curriculum. In effect, how could I, over the next few years, make myself redundant?!

Early days of planning

The first stage was to arm myself with the medium term planning for each year group in order to focus my work on the curriculum areas being covered. I began by drawing on my teaching experience both in schools and at the field studies centre to come up with some ideas, but also did various internet searches.

This is when I began to realise that, although I wasn't on my own, trying to find outdoor learning ideas linked to the curriculum for junior aged children was a challenging prospect. For busy teachers, trawling the internet for ideas that were disparate and spread few and far between was not a good use of time. It underlined the fact that a lack of ideas was a real barrier to teachers trying to use outdoor learning as a useful pedagogic approach. The longer term aim of developing my own website was hatched – but there was obviously the more immediate goal of planning for the first term!

In addition to using medium term planning, I looked at the grounds. I wandered, sat, dug, explored, thought, looked… Our grounds are big enough, but not huge. But I had read somewhere that it's a case of making the most of what you've got, not yearning for what isn't there (that could come later as part of a grounds development plan). So I mentally, and then on paper, zoned the grounds and the resources and opportunities they offered, and ideas and plans started to develop.

The day to day experiences

Having developed teaching and learning ideas, I then had to consider the logistics of taking learning outside on a regular basis. This obviously had wider implications than simply thinking about myself and the children. We informed parents as there would be times when the children would go home a little (or a lot) dirty, and it was important that parents understood why. We also had to consider how to make sure we didn't bring dirt back into the school so the cleaners weren't upset. Texts were sent home asking for wellies and coats to be brought in when necessary, with the back-up of PE shoes for those who forgot or didn't have any. Spare wellies were donated and a number of extra coats were also useful.

I had numerous conversations with our site manager about how I wanted to use the grounds, what resources I needed and how we could work together to ensure sustainability. It was time well spent as we developed a shared understanding and he would then come to me from time to time to make suggestions. The site manager has since moved on and we now have a new one – a few years into the process. The conversations will this time be a lot easier as I have a better idea of the needs of the children and the spaces we use. The initial, experimental phase has left us in a position of knowledge and strength in respect of where and how we want to progress from here.

Moving forward

As we moved into the second and third term and then years two and three, planning got easier and many of the ideas outlined in the main section of this book were developed. Having said that, there were many things we did in the first couple of years that haven't made it into this book, even though they were exciting and enjoyable learning experiences. I try to keep ideas fresh by adding in new elements so I don't feel I am churning out 'the same old' every year. And even elements that are repeated are tweaked and improved.

But having established the work with the children, I had time to turn some of my energies to looking at the whole-school approach. I ran a couple of staff meetings to explain the theory behind the practice and had some practical examples for staff to try out. The Deputy (in the Head's absence) then set out the longer term vision of staff looking more creatively at where teaching was to take place, with the expectation that more outdoor learning would happen. We also, at this stage, developed our own definition of outside learning:

Learning outside the classroom at Anstey Junior School includes any learning which is inspired by or takes place in a location alternative to the classroom. This includes using the school grounds or resources from it, day visits, residential visits, and visitors into school.

Although this didn't have much impact at the time, it was a useful exercise to ensure all staff were part of the process of arriving at a definition, rather than having one imposed on them. It also meant a policy could be drawn up and shared with governors to include them in the process and ensure support. The definition of outdoor learning is different to most you will see if you search on the internet. As a staff, we recognised that part of the reason for developing outdoor learning was to make the curriculum more interesting and engaging. The way to do this was obviously to take children outside, but there was also value in bringing the outside into the classroom, either things or people. This definition gave us the breadth to be able to explore these opportunities too.

We also planned an outdoor learning week where the traditional timetable was to be suspended, teachers were to spend time working in the school grounds with their classes, and I would arrange for a variety of visitors to come into school to work with the children (most of whom were free). I also liaised with our local teacher training university and arranged for a number of students to come and support us during the week, allowing teachers to plan learning opportunities knowing they would have extra pairs of hands to help. This really was a win-win arrangement with trainee teachers benefitting from the experience as much as our teachers and children.

So, within the first year, all children had an entitlement to outdoor learning with me once a fortnight, teachers were encouraged to use the grounds and we had an outdoor learning week. This was all in addition to a range of off-site visits to enhance topics and visitors coming into school to work with the children.

The following couple of years saw more formal and informal intervention by me, the Head and the senior leadership team (SLT). This included in parts of Inset days and more staff meetings, continuing to drip feed the positives and finding ways to overcome barriers. However, the process of developing outside learning is not an easy one, especially when put alongside all the other changes and initiatives that happen within schools and demands put upon teachers on a daily basis. I remember having contact with a Headteacher in Lincolnshire who was much further along the process: he warned it would take time and perseverance. How true! Even with a very willing and talented staff, evidence of classes learning outside was still patchy during the first two years.

So, what next? More time together as a staff when I had some input into the planning process, looking with teachers at medium term and weekly grids and investigating the best ways to identify outside learning opportunities in the early stages, rather than trying to find opportunities as the term developed. As always, the staff were enthusiastic and very innovative in their approach and thinking; they were able to identify opportunities when the best place to learn different concepts was outside in the school grounds.

And little by little, I began to see increasing amounts of evidence of outside learning. There was chalk on the playground, piles of sticks, clipboards missing from the outside learning cupboard, the welly shed was in a mess… some things that might have been annoying, but I was overwhelmingly delighted as it meant teachers had been outside with their children. These were absolute and discernible steps in the right direction!

The result of one Inset was that all class teachers had to come and observe their class working with me outside. A lot of pressure – eight extra observations in a half term – but a very valuable and interesting experience. Feedback was that teachers found it eye-opening and saw specific children working in very different ways and with different work partners than they would inside. There were comments about levels of commitment and engagement, about attitudes to problem solving and developing their own challenges. Many teachers remarked on the children's independence and their ability to resource their own learning. There were lots of questions which had the added benefit of making me think and explain. The process reinforced to me that having two teachers working together is a powerful combination where, in a supportive environment, both can and should benefit hugely.

But, as with many initiatives, there needs to be a reminder every so often in order to keep them at the forefront of people's minds. So, as part of my performance management, with support of the SLT and having run the idea past a couple of teachers first, I introduced outdoor learning books into all classrooms. A nominated child would have the role of recording any outside learning in the book, noting date, subject area and a brief description of the learning. The aim was to have a record, but not to add to the workload of the teacher. The result was that outside learning has developed as more of a focus than it had previously, with some teachers actually getting quite competitive. The children also took the lead in reminding teachers if they hadn't been learning outside recently. It was an easy introduction that meant no extra work for teachers, but had a positive response.

Next steps

The radical next step for our school would be for me to stop doing outside learning and hand it over entirely to the teachers. Planning for outside learning for all topics is now done (although it will be added to as inspiration strikes), resources are prepared and the grounds have been developed enough for class teachers to proceed. However, I don't think that is going to happen just yet. There are too many other demands and initiatives currently to take such a big step. So, I think for now I continue teaching outside. I have time with new staff to ensure they are aware of our approach and buy into it and I showcase new ideas through my website (which is linked to the school website) and displays in school.

In addition, I will aim to further raise the profile of the school with regards to outdoor learning by continuing to: run training courses (independently and for Hampshire County Council); develop further contacts with our link university; update my website, Facebook and Twitter feeds; keep up to date with educational research in this field. I will also use these resources to continually develop my practice to ensure the children I teach benefit from all the positives that outside learning brings them academically, socially and personally.

Lessons to be learned

There are various conclusions I have drawn from our work at Anstey:

- Change takes time. Even with willing and able staff, new initiatives, however important and worthy, will take time. There are so many pressures on teachers that developing a new, whole-school approach to something (especially if it isn't maths or English) will be hard and require perseverance.

- Drip feeding is important. However important the formal CPD sessions are, drip feeding ideas and resources on a regular basis can keep initiatives in the forefront of people's minds, thus continuing to keep them alive.
- Individuals make a difference. Although I believe that a whole-school approach to most initiatives like outdoor learning is preferable, it is possible for individual teachers to introduce outdoor learning to their classes and make a difference to that cohort of children. As the teacher of your own class, if you think it is important that children can learn outside, I would have that you could give it a go. Explain to your line manager with the evidence of research and try.

2 Science Outdoors

What does the National Curriculum say?

The National Curriculum Purpose of Study for science at key stages 1 and 2 states the following:

A high-quality science education provides the foundations for understanding the world through the specific disciplines of biology, chemistry and physics. Science has changed our lives and is vital to the world's future prosperity, and all pupils should be taught essential aspects of the knowledge, methods, processes and uses of science. Through building up a body of key foundational knowledge and concepts, pupils should be encouraged to recognise the power of rational explanation and develop a sense of excitement and curiosity about natural phenomena. They should be encouraged to understand how science can be used to explain what is occurring, predict how things will behave, and analyse causes.

The National Curriculum adds that the 'principal focus of science teaching in key stage 1 is to enable pupils to experience and observe phenomena, looking more closely at the natural and humanly constructed world around them'. This is developed at Years 3 and 4 where the 'principal focus of science teaching in lower key stage 2 is to enable pupils to broaden their scientific view of the world around them'. At the older end of key stage 2, the emphasis is placed on developing 'a deeper understanding of a wide range of scientific ideas'.

I would suggest that if science is to 'provide the foundations for understanding the world' then taking children outside into the world to learn ought to be important. In order to develop 'a sense of excitement and curiosity about natural phenomena', children need to be exposed to nature and the world around us, seeing science in its natural state. This will surely lead to children having the knowledge, experience and curiosity to 'explain what is occurring, predict how things will behave, and analyse causes'. Using the outside environment will allow children to practically challenge hypotheses, question ideas and learn in a practical and meaningful manner. As with other curriculum areas, learning about science in the children's own environment allows them to learn in a more concrete manner before considering concepts that may be more abstract (such as evolution and inheritance in Year 6). A good example of this is investigating how mini-beasts are adapted to live in the school grounds before thinking about creatures which live in deserts or alternative locations.

I have also found that carrying out science work in the school grounds can have a phenomenal impact on the children's ownership of and pride in their local area, which can have important positive social consequences. The activities related to identification and classification (see page 18) will illustrate this concept well.

It is worth taking, on a large sheet of card, the key scientific words you want the children to be using when working outside, developing the idea of working scientifically through using correct vocabulary. Children find this empowering and it encourages them to work as scientists because they are speaking as one.

I have set this chapter out in line with how the National Curriculum suggests learning and teaching should be covered across the different year groups, but also by grouping the themes together. For example, I have grouped all the work on plants that are taught in Years 1, 2 and 3 together, so it is easy to see what has been covered before and what the children will be moving on to. I have also tried to draw out some of the links between the different strands within the science curriculum, as there is some overlap which can be exploited. This may not be totally in line with what you do as a school, or what your authority recommends (Hampshire LA suggest sound is taught in Year 6 instead of Year 4) but you will be able to make any necessary adjustments.

In addition to the lessons I have outlined, I have tried to suggest some extra investigations that can be carried out outside. These could be interesting especially for those children who have a sound grasp of the key ideas and need to have the opportunity to apply their knowledge. For these investigations, I have suggested which year groups they seem most appropriate for – but as with most investigations, they can be adapted to suit different ages and abilities.

As I have said before, use these ideas as starting points and do think how they will fit into your teaching progression over the course of a sequence of lessons. They may not be ground breaking, but will help to keep outside learning at the forefront of your thoughts, ideas and planning. Be especially aware of key information your children will need to know before working outside as this will obviously support them in developing understanding, using questions and testing hypotheses. Consider as well how you can use any information gleaned or data collected back in the classroom – there are rich opportunities to link science with English, maths, history, art, personal development learning (PDL)…

And finally, due to the breadth of the science curriculum across the two key stages, I haven't tried to give ideas for all areas of study – just the ones that I have tried and tested, or ideas I know others have tried and endorsed, and can therefore vouch for. But please don't let my ideas limit your enthusiasm or imagination!

Working scientifically

With a little forethought and planning, all the elements of working scientifically can be addressed when working outside: sessions can be planned that focus on asking and answering questions. Magnifying glasses and hoops can be used to focus observation skills; tests can be carried out; charts can be used to support identification and classification; key questions can be answered based on observations and experiences; and information can be gathered in a number of ways.

My suggestion would be to be explicit about which of the elements of working scientifically you are concentrating on, making sure there is plenty of time for coverage and revisiting over the two year span. Different activities will lend themselves to a different 'working scientifically' focus, so it is worth identifying it in your planning. On one occasion, having asked children to observe and find different leaves growing in the field, I soon realised that they didn't necessarily have the skills needed to observe carefully and scientifically. We came back together, talked about and practiced by getting on our hands and knees, parting the grass, looking for different leaf types and using magnifying glasses, before sending the children off to work more independently. The difference in the quality of the children's findings was huge. So do be explicit and teach the scientific skills necessary, especially when you realise there may be a deficit.

Plants: Year 1

Identifying plants

Learning objective
'Identify and name a variety of common wild and garden plants, including deciduous and evergreen trees.'

Cross-curricular links
English, maths, art

Soft skills development
Attention to detail, co-operation, observation

Resources
Identification charts, camera, recording sheets, double-sided sticky tape, pencils, clipboards

Identifying different plants and trees from their leaves

What to do
The types of identification charts you need will very much depend on your location. Buy, print or even better, create ones that you know will allow the children to work successfully with specific trees and plants on them that you wish to be identified. Determining plants using leaves is often a good way to work, but depending on the time of year, buds and flowers may also be an option.

Armed with recording sheets that could look like this one, cut to the size you require, and take the children outside to find leaves and identify the plants or trees they have come from.

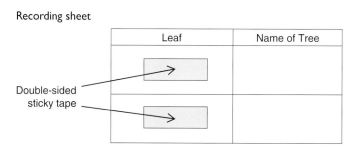
Recording sheet

Leaf	Name of Tree

Double-sided sticky tape

If you wish to develop this work in a cross-curricular manner, you can also include some measuring by looking at the number of different sorts of leaves that have been found (data collection), some rubbings and line drawings... there are many different opportunities.

Structure of common flowering plants

Learning objective
Identify and describe the basic structure of a variety of common flowering plants, including trees.

Cross-curricular links
English, maths, art

Soft skills development
Attention to detail, co-operation, observation, care, team work

Resources
Identification charts, camera, paper, magnifying glasses, pencils

Observing plants in their natural habitats before investigating their structure

What to do
Most schools have some grass and growing areas – but if you don't, plan ahead and plant some seeds or bulbs in pots so they will be ready for when you need them. It is good to have a variety of different plants so children can compare and contrast. If you have a field, then you are likely to have grass, dandelions, clover and daisies at least and perhaps many more.

Identifying the plants you are going to be investigating is good practice as the children are then more able to use the correct names and work more scientifically. If at all possible, take the children outside to select and dig their own plants (depending on the weather, you may need to water an area of the field to make digging easier). Encourage the children to work with care as they want the whole plant, and not just the bit the can see. Don't take for granted that the children know what is below the ground. If your children don't know, ask them to pull at the grass and discuss why they can't pull it up.

Once plants have been dug, lay them out on paper and ask the children to look really closely at what they can see. Label the main parts (flower, stem, leaf, roots) and ask them to describe what they look like and create some discussion about the purpose. Notes can be made on the sheets along with the labels and then take photos of their work as evidence.

All of this work can be done outside, reducing mess in the classroom! It is also nice in the classroom to have plants growing – bulbs in a clear glass containers – so the process can be seen: cress, starting tomato plants, salad leaves, chitting potatoes… the list is endless.

I have also organised a whole-school bulb planting with bulbs donated by parents and a local supermarket (who also provided their Community Liaison Lead to come and help!). Cutting a daffodil bulb open and looking closely is really interesting too – and we did a quiz around the grounds to show how bulbs grow (see the next idea).

Plants: Year 2

Observing plants

Learning objective
Observe and describe how seeds and bulbs grow into mature plants.

Cross-curricular links
English, maths

Soft skills development
Observation, explanation, co-operation

Resources
Bulbs, seeds, recording sheets, compost, pots/seed trays, quiz cards

What to do
In addition to planting seeds and bulbs and measuring the growth over time (either in terms of height and/or number of seeds that germinate) children like to see, using pictures or time-lapse videos, what is going to happen. Make a series of numbered cards with pictures and explanations on, showing and explaining the way bulbs or seeds grow. Hang these up around the school grounds. The children then have recording sheets with either corresponding pictures or numbers. The children have to find the cards and fill in the given information on their cards. If they work in pairs, they can support each other with the reading and writing if necessary.

This activity can be easily differentiated by, for example, having key words highlighted, or the children could just have to fill in the missing words on their recording sheet. I also have two sets of information cards – a simpler version printed on white, and a more detailed option printed on yellow. They are hung up together but you can direct the children to the one they should look at.

Living plants

Learning objective
Find out and describe how plants need water, light and a suitable temperature to grow and stay healthy.

I won't go into detail about this topic as I think most are confident in investigate conditions needed for plant growth. I would say that investigating plant growth in the school grounds is a natural environment and the children will then be able to relate their learning in school to the wider locality in which they live.

This learning objective only asks the children to understand what is needed for plants to grow and stay healthy, so looking at the grass on the school field and other plants and trees around the grounds will provide opportunities for asking and answering questions.

It is also interesting to see what happens when grass is deprived of light by covering a patch with black plastic sheeting, bin bags or similar. An arrangement of bricks would also suffice. Look at the impact this has on the grass over a period of time, but also note the resilience of grass to recover from such deprivation. Do consider whether the grass is just being deprived of light, or if it is being deprived of water too. Creating a test which addresses both could be done using black plastic bags for light and water, clear plastic sheeting for just light, and black weed repellent for water.

I do think we are missing a trick though if, during a topic about plants, we don't support the children in growing food crops, especially if space is limited and you aren't able to have a growing programme in your school. Salad crops and flowers can easily be planted and looked after in pots, and allow you to place them in a convenient location – and are only a temporary fixture so you are less likely to get complaints from the powers that be! This will allow the children to consider how, having investigated plants that are currently growing, they can ensure their own plants and seeds have access to the correct levels of water and light and the right temperature to grow.

Understanding how to grow and care for plants

Plants: Year 3

Identifying and describing plants

Learning objective
Identify and describe the functions of different parts of flowering plants: roots, stem/trunk, leaves and flowers.

Cross-curricular links
Art

Soft skill development
Observation skills, explanation, drawing conclusions

Resources
Large bits of paper, trowels, pencils, magnifying glasses, straws

What to do
This element builds directly on from work in Year 2 when the children identify parts of a flowering part. The development is that, in Year 3, children need to describe the functions of each part of the plant.

I would, again, take the children outside and ask them to dig up dandelions, daisies or other common plants that are growing in your school grounds. If these aren't available, then plan ahead and grow some flowering plants in pots so they can be 'decanted' and dissected for the children to investigate.

Stay outside if possible to reduce mess in the classroom, have the plants on large paper and encourage the children to investigate them closely with magnifying glasses. They can annotate what they see, and this will give you the chance to see what the children have recalled from their learning in Year 1 in terms of parts of plants, before you move on.

Developing an understanding of different parts of the plants can be part instruction and part experimentation. For example, when discussing roots, have the children pull at some grass and ask why it won't come out of the ground easily. Give the children straws and cups of water to illustrate one of the roles of a stem. (This will then link to work on how water is transported in plants, which is well illustrated by putting light coloured flowers in water with food dye added).

Work on the role of different parts of plans can be added to the annotations, perhaps in a different colour to show the difference between naming parts and descriptions. Photos can be taken to add to science books for evidence.

The close observation in this work means that the children would be in a good position to develop their ideas into art work, which could be further inspired by the work of Georgia O'Keefe.

Living plants and how they vary

Learning objective
Explore the requirements of plants for life and growth (air, light, water, nutrients from soil, and room to grow) and how they vary from plant to plant.

Cross-curricular links
English, maths

Soft skill development
Observation, attention to detail, team work and collaboration, communication

Resources
Plants or seeds, pots, growing media, water, measuring jugs, scales

What to do
Developing on from the ideas from Year 2 that identify the elements needed for plant growth, this learning objective asks children to experiment with the different conditions.

I think we are all good at supporting children in developing experiments to see what happens if different amount of light or water are given to plants. However, it is even more interesting to put the investigation into a context. For example, seeds were sent into space last year. We all know that seeds need water to grow, and too little water will prevent germination and too much will drown the seed. So rather than carrying out an experiment to prove what is already known, can the children investigate what the optimum amount of water is to send into space to make sure certain seeds grow? This is a crucial investigation as carrying too much water into space will have an impact on space and weight within the space craft. Results can then be sent to the European Space Agency – you may well get a reply!

This is just one example of a contextualised experiment which will mean more to the children, and which means they are actually investigating something real.

Another 'real-life scenario' would be to study the effect of light and water on grass growth here (see page 21) and link it to any school grounds developments being considered, and what impact that may have on plant growth.

In any investigation of this type, make sure you have the resources needed, and support the children in working scientifically, encouraging fair testing, detailed observation, and measuring and recording when necessary.

Life cycle of plants

Learning objective
Explore the part that flowers play in the life cycle of flowering plants, including pollination, seed formation and seed dispersal.

Cross-curricular links
Maths

Soft skills development
Accuracy, turn taking, co-operation

Resources
Straws, scissors, seeds (the right size to fit inside the straws), metre sticks, chalk, balloons

What to do
Investigating seed dispersal gives the children a great chance to experiment with fair testing – a lot of children are very good at identifying the features of fair testing, but putting it into practice can be a bit more of a challenge. The quality of the results in this investigation may not sometimes be as valuable as the process and the children's experiences – but the debate around why this is the case is also valuable.

There is a brilliant video on BBC Bitesize illustrating the main methods of seed dispersal (see Bibliography for link) which is worth watching first, and then these experiments focus on the explosion method.

The children are going to find out whether a longer or shorter straw makes the seed disperse further. By drawing a starting point on the playground, the children blow a seed out of a straw to see how far it goes. Mark where it lands with chalk. Repeat this three times to ensure it is a fair test, and let each child have a go (working in groups of three works quite well as you can have a blower, a spotter and a marker!).

The seeds can be quite difficult to spot, but the children do get better at it – however, do let them 'play' first to get their eye in, and have plenty of seeds for those that can't be found.

Cut the straw shorter and repeat. Mark the results on the playground in different coloured chalk from the first set to allow comparisons to be more easily made. The straw can be cut again to a third length if required.

Results can be measured and recorded and graphs made if you want to exploit the links with maths, although the results on the playground are clear enough to discuss.

What is important though is to discuss the elements of the test that are fair and those which are more difficult to control; the most important one being the strength of the breath. The children may also suggest the wind will impact on the results – but there is an argument to say that these elements are replicating the conditions seeds will encounter in real life.

A further way to look at explosion is to screw up some 'paper seeds' very small and put the same number (about 20) into three different balloons. You could use different coloured paper for each balloon to help with comparisons later. Blow the balloons up to different sizes, one small, one medium and one large. Ask the children to predict which 'seeds' will disperse further when the balloons are burst. Take each balloon in turn, stand in the same place each time, with the balloon held at the same height (but ask the children to identify these fair testing features), pop the balloon and see where the seeds end up. Discuss what the results show and whether conclusions can be drawn. This may or may not be possible, but again the discussions about what's happened are worth having.

Investigating explosive seed dispersal using balloons - great fun!

Plant investigations

- Does the size of the seed planted effect the size of the plant produced? (Year 1 and Year 2)
- Can you bring a plant back to life? – ask for donations of dying plants (from a garden centre or parents) and try to resurrect them. (Year 1 and Year 2)
- What's the best medium to grow seeds if there is no soil? (Year 3)
- Do plants in a greenhouse always grow quicker than those outside? You don't need a greenhouse to do this – just make cloches from plastic bottles. (Year 3)

Animals, including humans: Year 1

Identifying animals

Learning objectives
- Identify animals from different classes;
- Identify creatures that are omnivores, herbivores and carnivores;
- Describe and compare the structure of a variety of common animals (fish, amphibians, reptiles, birds and mammals, including pets).

This is one element of learning and teaching where you will have to check your school's risk assessment and list of allergies. Hand washing after exposure to animals is crucial. I would also be very wary about having any dogs in school, unless they are specifically trained to work with children (for example, the 'reading to dogs' scheme). I have grouped all these elements together as you can touch on all of them if you manage to organise to have some animals brought into school. Take photos and use them in subsequent lessons too.

Cross-curricular links
English, art, maths, PDL

Soft skills development
Empathy, care, observation, analysis, questioning

Resources
Photographs of different types of animals, real animals (pets that parents can bring in, ask a local pet store to bring some in for a couple of hours), magnifying glasses, camera, chalks

What to do
Arrange for some animals to be brought into your school grounds. If possible, select animals that the children can stroke and hold. You may have local contacts who have specific animals, but pet shops often have the facility to bring animals into school in return for a bit of publicity. There are also numerous mobile farms that you could try, which have the added benefit of having all the risk assessments done for you. We manage, even with more than 250 children in school, to make sure all children get time with the animals when we have a farm visit, reducing the cost to about £1 per child, which should be manageable.

Discussion around similarities and differences will enable the children to not only identify the creatures, but also allow children to begin to consider whether they are mammals, birds or reptiles and start the formal process of classification. What the animals eat can also be discussed, and then the scientific terms 'omnivore', 'herbivore' and 'carnivore' can be introduced and animals classified accordingly. Some reference can be made to teeth types, but this does come into the key stage 2 curriculum. Once the children have had hands-on experiences with animals, they may be able to look at pictures and draw comparisons between the images and what they have actually handled. Images can be identified and classified, with appropriate and correct scientific terminology being used.

Using a range of photos of animals that the children have actually handled, you could ask the children to group them according to different characteristics. They could also try to draw life size versions of them on the playground in chalk. You could give the children the heights of a range of different creatures and they could do a height chart on a school wall to show relative sizes.

Labelling the human body

Learning objective
Identify, name, draw and label the basic parts of the human body and say which part of the body is associated with each sense.

Cross-curricular links
English, art, maths, PDL

Soft skills development
Turn taking, attention to detail, co-operation

Resources
Chalks

What to do
Ask the children to work in twos or threes. One of the children lies down on the playground and the other draws round them as carefully as possible. Draw on the facial features. Then they can take it in turns to label the different parts of the body, going into as

Drawing then labelling the body

much detail as possible – challenge them to name a certain number of different parts, depending on their ability. Word cards can be provided for those who might find the spelling difficult, or make a class list with correct spellings as the children work so they can correct themselves.

Once the main labelling has been done, move onto the parts of the body that are associated with each sense. Work may have been done on this area previously, or this may introduce the topic.

Animals, including humans: Year 2

Animal needs

Learning objective
Find out about and describe the basic needs of animals, including humans, for survival (water, food and air).

Have a look at the ideas in the 'Year 2 Living things and their habitats' section of this chapter (see page 41) for ideas, as there is overlap between the two sections.

Healthy lifestyle
• Describe the importance for humans of exercise, eating the right amounts of different types of food, and hygiene.

Cross-curricular links
PE, maths

Soft skills development
Resilience, self-awareness

Resources
PE equipment, recording charts, marker pens

What to do
When doing PE lessons, encourage the children to see what impact exercise has on the body. You could have charts where children can record changes in skin colour and heart rate, if they sweat, when limbs start to feel tired, etc. In my experience, for some children, this needs to be explained as being a positive outcome!

Once the children have experienced and identified physical changes, it is possible to then explain how this is having a positive impact and how exercise, over a period of time, will have long term positive effects. It is worth repeating the process at the end of the term to see if fitness levels have risen, for example, has it taken longer for the limbs to ache than at the beginning of the term?

In terms of food, look at different food families. A balanced diet can be supported easily by growing and trying different foods that are produced within the school grounds. (This ties in with elements of the Plants curriculum, and even if you don't have a growing programme in school, you can still grow salad crops very easily and quickly.)

I would also ask a local supermarket if they would like to come and do some food tasting with children. There is one, which has a specific programme, and I have always found them very supportive of all initiatives that I have asked them to be involved in. They have come in on a regular basis with different foods along different themes to try, from breads and bagels to cheese and fruits, all fitting in with class topics.

Animals, including humans: Year 3

Human skeletons

Learning objective
Identify that humans and some other animals have skeletons and muscles for support, protection and movement.

Cross-curricular links
English, art, maths, PDL

Soft skills development
Attention to detail, co-operation, speaking and listening, negotiation

Resources
Sticks, chalk, copies of x-rays

Creating part of a skeleton requires real attention to detail

What to do
Having looked at a range of x-rays on the interactive whiteboard and for the children to discover which part of the body they are from or which animal they belong to, ask the children to create the bones in their hands from sticks. It is really informative to get the children to feel their hands, to recognise where their bones are, and to realise that bones connect to each other at joints. The sense of realisation of how many bones there are in the hand is amazing to see… children start to hypothesise how many bones there might be in the whole body – so interesting! (If you have time, before the following activity, ask the children to create a 'skeleton' of their hand and arm using sticks. It is a really interesting exercise that provides amble opportunity for talking about bones and joints.)

Then move on to working with chalks on the playground. Ask the children to work in small groups. One child is to lie on the floor and be drawn around, carefully. The task is to add all the bones in the right place. Have copies of x-rays of different parts of the body. The children first have to work out what part of the body they are, and then add the bones accurately to their diagram.

If you ask the children to do the bones in white chalk, you can then challenge them to add different organs in coloured chalk after finishing the skeleton. The learning, discussions and care in this activity can be amazing, with the children developing a really secure understanding of their skeleton (and organs) and how everything fits together.

This learning obviously involves lots of talking, but you can also develop it into measuring (maths), discussions about health (PDL) and even into 2D and 3D art work.

Animals, including humans: Year 4

The digestive system

Learning objective
Describe the simple functions of the basic parts of the digestive system in humans.

Cross-curricular links
English, PDL

Soft skills development
Attention to detail, co-operation, speaking and listening, negotiation

Resources
Chalks, biscuits, camera

What to do
As an Assessment for Learning task, ask the children to work in groups. Ask one child in each group to lie on the floor and draw around them. Give each group a biscuit that can be broken and shared (check any allergies). Each child eats their biscuit and has to think about where that biscuit goes, and what will happen to it over the next couple of days. Then challenge the children to show this on the body drawn on the playground. It is worth taking photos so you have 'before and after' photographic evidence, showing how much value you have added.

It is a great activity to understand what the children know and what you need to teach about digestion – but definitely worth repeating at the end of the unit so you can see how the children's understanding has developed. The second photos can be compared to the first – both you and the children will hopefully be really impressed!

Food chains

Learning objective
Construct and interpret a variety of food chains, identifying producers, predators and prey.

This develops work from Year 2 that is included in the 'Living things and their habitats' section.

Cross-curricular links
PDL

Soft skills development
Reasoning, logic, speaking and listening, negotiation

Resources
Pictures and/or toys of animals, chalks, key word list, specific pictures of animals and plants in a food chain

What to do
Do think about what prior information the children need to know before carrying out this activity.

Depending on prior experience and knowledge, I sometimes start by distributing a range of pictures with an animal or plant on the front and a habitat on the back. There maybe five or six different habitats, with four or five animals or plants from each one. The children need to get into habitat groups and then decide which order the plants and animals go in to show who eats what. Repeat the activity a few times, so the children get to know which living things come from which habitat, and how the food chains work.

Next, draw a sun in the middle of the playground and ask the children to construct food chains coming out from the sun, with the first item being a green plant. Children can start by drawing the food chains from the starting activity, and then add their own ideas from knowledge of pets or other animals. Once pictures are drawn on the playground, they can be labelled using the relevant words on the key word list which should include predator, prey, producer, but can also include herbivore, carnivore, omnivore (linking to work on teeth).

Once food chains have been developed, ask the children to look and see if the same creature has been included in different chains. Connect them and make a web instead of a chain and discuss the interdependence of all the creatures.

It is then quite interesting and relevant to consider what happens if, for example, something gets diseased, or the impact of the badger cull. Either rub out or cross out all instances of that type of creature, for example, badgers. Discuss what would happen to the animals that used to eat badgers (they wouldn't have enough to eat) and the creatures the badgers used to eat (their numbers would increase).

Animals, including humans: Year 6

Circulatory system

Learning objective
Identify and name the main parts of the human circulatory system, and describe the functions of the heart, blood vessels and blood.

Cross-curricular links
PDL

Soft skills development
Team work, co-operation, communication

Resources
Chalk, blue and red cards

What to do
Do some preparatory work so the children know the specific vocabulary and have a basic understanding of how the circulatory system works and what it looks like. Work with your class to draw the outline of a body on the playground, as large as you possibly can. Draw on the heart, lungs, brain, and some of the veins and arteries.

The actual learning activity is quite hard to explain but have a read and see if you can make it work for you. It is worth persevering with, I promise!

The children then create a working model of the circulatory system. Position the children at different points around the body, and those closest to the heart move around holding red cards, as the blood is full of oxygen at this stage. As they move around the body, they have to exchange red cards for blue ones that show that the amount of oxygen in the blood is reducing. More oxygen can come into the body all the time through breathing, so once they are back at the heart, more oxygen (red cards) are available. The class has to work together to make sure there is enough oxygen and that it gets to all parts of the body.

You can change the dynamics by suggesting that the body is asleep, or exercising. Discuss with the children what impact this would have on breathing levels, heart rate and blood flow, and see how they represent this in their working model.

Healthy lifestyle

Learning objective
Recognise the impact of diet, exercise, drugs and lifestyle on the way their bodies function

Cross-curricular links
PDL, PE, maths

Soft skills development
Team work, leadership, support and encouragement

Resources
Cones, stop watch, recording sheets, metre sticks or trundle wheel

What to do
It is relatively easy to practically look at the effect of exercise and possibly diet on the ways our bodies function (whereas the effects of drugs will be looked at in other ways). Children can keep food diaries and you can work with them and their families to look at the benefits of eating a balanced diet and drinking enough water.

With exercise, however, you can be more scientific and carry out tests to measure and record changes over time. The Cooper test involves seeing how many times you can run round a square of a given distance in a certain time. The Bleep test is running backwards and forwards between cones with the time you have to complete each lap getting shorter each time.

With both of these tests, children can work together to count the number of laps, or the number of 'bleeps' completed at the beginning of a term, and then repeat it at intervals during the term to see if they are improving. In order to improve, they will need to consider what types of exercise they are going to do between the tests, and perhaps keep a record of this too.

Water and nutrients

Learning objective
Describe the ways in which nutrients and water are transported within animals, including humans.

Cross-curricular links
PDL, English

Soft skills development
Team work, attention to detail, thinking skills, speaking and listening, negotiation

Resources
Chalks, water bottles

What to do
As an Assessment for Learning task, ask the children to work in groups. Ask one child in each group to lie on the playground floor and draw around them. Then ask each child to take a drink of water, and ask the children to consider what happens to the water as it moves through the body. There are fundamental differences between what happens to water and food, including perspiration. Next, challenge the children to show this on the body drawn on the playground.

These drawings, and the accompanying conversations, will let you know what level of understanding the children have. The activity can be carried out either at the beginning of your teaching, or at the end as an assessment – or both!

Animals, including humans investigations

- How do animals see in the dark? There are lots of blindfold games that can be played and developed into investigations to try to imagine how to sense danger. (Year1 and Year 2)
- Where would the best place be in the school grounds for an egg to hatch? It could be a bird's egg, but it may not be. Come up with suggestions for a blackbird and a tortoise. (Year 1 and Year 2)
- Hide some bones in the school grounds (ask a butcher for some and clean them thoroughly first!) for the children to explore, find and investigate. What can they find out from the bones about the creature it can from? What other equipment would they need to find out more? (Year 3 and Year 4)
- Is there a difference between the effect prolonged gentle exercise and interval training has on heart rate? (Year 5 and Year 6)

Materials: Year 1

Objects and materials

Learning objectives
- Distinguish between an object and the material from which it is made;
- Identify and name a variety of everyday materials, including wood, plastic, glass, metal, water, and rock;
- Describe the simple physical properties of a variety of everyday materials;
- Compare and group together a variety of everyday materials on the basis of their simple physical properties.

Again, I have addressed these elements together as there is a lot of overlap. The ideas suggested below can be carried out in 'lesson blocks' or as a whole morning/day immersion, whatever bests suits you and your children.

Cross-curricular links
English, art, maths

Soft skills development
Observation, team work, collaboration, listening

Resources
Hoops, chalk, collections of materials and objects, camera

What to do
Looking at objects and what they are made from can happen during a walk around the school grounds, as well as working with things within the classroom. Before you go out, have an idea of what you want the children to discover so you can guide the walk, but I am sure the children will also find things they want to investigate. You could make a recording sheet using names of objects or photos with the children having to identify what each object is made from, or you could just let them find their own objects. Rather than using a recording sheet, you could give children labels with the words 'plastic', 'wood', 'glass' etc. written on them and ask the children to sticky tack them onto different objects.

Once objects and materials have been looked at in context, a collection of different materials can be presented to the children to sort. You can draw Venn Diagrams or Carroll Diagrams on the playground or use PE hoops. Ask the children to sort either according to their own criteria, or criteria that you give them. The children can also collect their own objects, or even draw or write things into different sets so you can see if they can extend their knowledge and understanding more independently.

Materials: Year 2

Everyday materials

Learning objective
Identify and compare the suitability of a variety of everyday materials, including wood, metal, plastic, glass, brick, rock, paper and cardboard for particular uses.

Cross-curricular links
English, maths, art

Soft skills development
Observation, explanation, developing ideas

Resources
Recording sheets, pencils, clipboards

What to do
Walking around the school grounds will provide you with a wide variety of objects made from different materials. You could use a recording sheet similar to the one described in Year 1 where an object and the material it is made from is identified, but this time add a column to explain why it's the best material.

Alternatively, you could have a class chart, or let the more able children do their own and have a group one for those who might struggle with recording their ideas. Or, if you don't need written evidence, you could just talk about the findings.

To further investigate the suitability of materials for different jobs, encourage the children to talk about or draw what objects would be like if they were made of different materials. Imagine if the whole playground was grass, or if the adventure playground was made out of brick. This activity leads to some very interesting discussions and ideas!

Materials investigations

- What is the best material to make a mini-greenhouse for a plant? Can you prove it and explain why? (Year 1 and 2)
- Test different materials to decide which is the best choice to make a roof tile. (Year 1 and 2)
- We want to keep some soft toys outside for playtime games. How can we keep them in a good condition? (Year 1 and 2)
- My umbrella has a hole in it. What's the best material to make a patch to mend it? (Year 1 and 2)

States of matter: Year 4

The water cycle

Learning objective
Identify the part played by evaporation and condensation in the water cycle and associate the rate of evaporation with temperature.

There is obviously a big link between science and geography in this element of work, and I think it is important that the overlaps are made explicit. Using geographical knowledge can also allow hypotheses to be made and investigations to be carried out.

Cross-curricular links
English, maths, geography

Soft skills development
Observation, attention to detail, thinking skills, communication

Resources
Water, chalk, metre sticks or tape measures, camera, pegs, tea towel cut into small pieces, sticks, wool, copies of the Beaufort scale

What to do
If you have time, observe what happens to real puddles over the course of a day, recording their size with chalk and measuring at set time intervals. Ask the children why the size of the puddle has changed. What are the environmental factors that have affected the size? Having identified that it may be the sun and wind that make the water evaporate, you can then set up fair tests creating puddles with equal amounts of water in different places in the grounds. Observe and measure where puddles evaporate more quickly and what conclusions you can draw about the different environmental conditions.

Also, set the children the challenge to find the best place to locate a washing line for the kitchen staff to hang their tea towels so that they dry really quickly. Using maps of the grounds, the children test wind speed (by making their own 'wind socks' with a stick and wool tied to one end) and compare it to the Beaufort Scale. They can also mark sun and shade spots after lunch, when the tea towels would need hanging out. They then suggest the best 5 or 6 places, and hang pieces of wet tea towel with a few going back to check on progress every half hour. The results can be written up and presented to the kitchen staff.

Rocks: Year 3

Learning about rocks

Learning objectives
- Compare and group together different kinds of rocks on the basis of their appearance and simple physical properties;
- Recognise that soils are made from rocks and organic matter.

Cross-curricular links
Art, history

Soft skills development
Observation, team work, collaboration, organisation

Working as a group to see what's in a pot of soil

Resources
A variety of rocks and stones, sieves, magnifying glasses, marker pens, water, vinegar, straws (or pipettes), large card, nails, recording sheets, paint palettes, water, paint brushes, masking tape, rolling pins (or similar for crushing rocks), paper

What to do
Take the children outside to dig in soil and see what they can find. I had assumed that the children would already have had this experience, but it appears that many hadn't so this is an important activity. Having done this independently, provide the children with a plant pot of soil. Ask them to separate all the different components on a piece of card and label the different things they can identify. Draw conclusions about what soil is made of.

Look at a range of rocks, describe and group them according to properties decided on by the children. Allow them to explain their choices. The rocks can be locally sourced or from further afield, or a mixture of the two. Do make it clear that different rocks occur in different locations, and not all can be found everywhere. Lava is the perfect example that can be explained easily. Allow the children to test rocks for hardness (using a nail to scratch), porosity (dropping water) and reaction to acid (dropping vinegar). Set up stations with all the required resources and allow the children to experiment and observe. Results can be recorded individually or you can collate children's findings as a class, and discuss which is the hardest and softest rock, which are porous, etc.

To help the children really understand that there are different types of rocks and soil, you can also use them to make paints. Have a selection of soils from different places (garden, compost, clay based, sand based) and some rocks that can be crashed or squashed (chalk or limestone, hardened clay…). Ask the children to make paints by mixing the soils with a little water, or by crushing the rocks first then mixing with water. Section off paper using masking tape and paint each section with different paint. If you are combining this unit with a Stone Age theme, you can also use the paints to do cave paintings either on long pieces of backing paper, or directly onto a wall (knowing it will get washed off when it rains!).

Fossils

Learning objective
Describe in simple terms how fossils are formed when things that have lived are trapped within rock.

Cross-curricular links
Art

Soft skills development
Attention to detail, observation, organisation

Resources
Video, pencils, booklets, crayons, examples of fossils (or photos if you haven't got the real things)

What to do
Share out fossils and pictures of fossils on tables and let the children explore them. It will give you a chance to see who the 'experts' are and talk to the children about their current knowledge. Having let the children have a look at the real things, use a really good animated video from YouTube which illustrates different types of fossils and how they are made (see Bibliography for link). The children can then combine this information with what they have seen on their tables, which can be really powerful.

Confirm that one of the features of fossils is that they once had to be alive – which links with previous work in science about living and non-living things. Take the children outside with notebooks (made from folded A5 paper) and ask them to draw or make rubbings of things within the school grounds that may become fossils in the future. The children love exploring and we have found sap that can make resin fossils, as well as doing leaf and bark rubbings and drawings of different creatures.

Seasonal change: Year 1

Observing the seasons

Learning objective
Observe changes across the four seasons.

On the surface seasonal change seems quite straightforward, but in order for the 'change' part to be meaningful the children have to have a recollection of what places are like over time. For some young children, this can be a challenge. This is one area where I would definitely recommend some sort of recording of outside experiences so that children can be reminded of what a certain place was like in a previous season. Photos and videos are important to provide a visual recollection, but some way of including children's thoughts and feelings, measurements or other recordings will also add to the experience and provide more opportunities for cross-curricular links. I would also consider looking at change on a monthly basis, and then linking the months to seasons – looking only four times a year would leave too long a gap for the experiences to be meaningful.

Cross-curricular links
English, maths, art

Soft skills development
Observation, questioning, attention to detail

Resources
Camera, iPad or other recording device, recording sheets, books, white sheet, magnifying glasses

What to do
What you do will depend very much on your environment and location but I would suggest that observing one area within your grounds over a school year is a good way to start. You could pick, for example, the first Friday of each month that you are in school and decide what you want to record and measure. To give a concrete example, if you were to pick a specific tree, you could:

- Take photos so leaf coverage can be compared.
- Measure the girth at a certain point.
- Measure the length of leaves.
- Record the colour of the leaves.
- Investigate if there is any buds, seeds or fruit.
- Use a sheet to collect anything living in the leaves by shaking a branch over a white sheet and identify and quantify what's there.
- Record the weather – temperature, cloud cover, wind strength, rain/snow.
- Collect thoughts and feelings when the children sit under the tree – this will be influenced by the weather, but could also include other thoughts and feelings written on sticky notes.
- Children draw what they can see, do rubbings, or collect items and make a collage.

Keep the recordings in a specific class book (rather than the children's own books) to make the information easier to compare. Each month, it is worth looking back at previous recordings before going out again.

Living things and their habitats: Year 2

This section will involve finding and observing mini-beasts. Please ensure that your children do so with care, making sure that nothing is harmed in their work and creatures are returned safely to where they were found.

If your school doesn't have an area where creatures live, either explore your local area to see if you can take children off site, or try to create your own micro-habitat. Some soil (an open grow bag if necessary), a couple of logs, some plants (even in pots) and some turf will encourage some creatures – just plan ahead!

Habitats and micro-habitats

Learning objective
Identify and name a variety of plants and animals in their habitats, including micro-habitats.

Cross-curricular links
Maths, art

Soft skills development
Observation, justification and explanation, attention to detail

Resources
Identification cards – can be specifically made to suit your environment (better for lower ability children), or more general ones that the children have to select species from (adds more of a challenge), magnifying glasses

What to do
Give the children time to explore certain areas of the school grounds – they will probably need some time to simply delight in what they can find before you introduce any formal identification.

Identification charts can be used purely to identify, or can be designed to enable children to record how many of each thing they can find. This gives you some data to use back in the classroom. The close observation skills needed to make positive identification can also be transferred into some beautiful pencil and pen drawings, and further developed into watercolour artwork.

Different habitats

Learning objective
Identify that most living things live in habitats to which they are suited, and describe how habitats provide for the basic needs of different kinds of animals and plants and how they depend on each other.

This learning objective links directly to the one form the 'Animals, including humans' section, which discusses their basic needs.

Cross-curricular links
PDL, Design Technology (DT)

Soft skills development
Empathy and understanding, negotiation, explanation

Resources
Magnifying glasses, paper towels, laminated maps of the school grounds, white board pens

What to do
Before going outside, it is worth talking with the children about what basic needs all animals have (food, water, shelter, reproduction) – Maslow's Pyramid can be used for this and is, I think, appropriate for younger children as well as older ones. Initially, the children could make their own pyramids using pictures you give them, or by drawing their own – it would be interesting to see which elements they think are essentials and how this compares to Maslow.

Having identified creatures (either previously or as part of this session), the children could be challenged to find where creatures would find food, water and protection (paper towels can be used to assess the moisture content of the area you are investigating). If required for evidence, findings can be recorded on maps of the school grounds.

You could then explore alternative, more barren areas, and ask why creatures don't live there and what elements necessary for survival are missing. This could even lead to a plan to improve and enhance the school grounds – even small features like adding bird feeders help the children to realise that they can make a difference (there are numerous options for bird feeders that the children can make themselves which are great).

Food chains and food sources

Learning objective
Describe how animals obtain their food from plants and other animals using the idea of a simple food chain, and identify and name different sources of food.

Cross-curricular links
PDL

Soft skills development
Thinking, co-operation, reasoning and explanation

Resources
Chalks, pictures that connect together to make food chains – or masks

What to do
Drawing food chains on strips of paper can be a lovely end product and supports development of fine motor skills, as well as scientific understanding. But asking children to make physical food chains outside in the playground – either holding pictures, wearing masks, or using models or toys – is a lovely thing to do. It provides many more opportunities for communication and discussion.

It is also good to get the children to draw food chains on the playground. If you start by drawing the sun in the middle, have the children, in groups (probably), draw a green plant of some sort. Put the arrows to connect (in the right direction), and then they develop the food chain from there. The finished diagram on the playground gets the children to start to appreciate how 'big' nature is.

Food chains that are then drawn on paper (if they are still deemed necessary) tend to be developed much more independently as the children build on their outside, practical experiences.

Living things and their habitats: Year 4

Identifying and classifying living things

Learning objectives
- Explore and use classification keys to help group, identify and name a variety of living things in their local and wider environment;
- Recognise that living things can be grouped in a variety of ways.

Cross-curricular links
Maths, art

Soft skills development
Care, observation, logic

Resources
Collecting dishes, magnifying glasses, recording sheet (either a class, group, or individual one)

Searching for invertebrates in order to identify and classify them

What to do
This follows on beautifully from the identification work in Year 2, but the children might well need time to remind themselves of this prior learning. Once you are happy with the children's ability to identify, you can start to classify.

If time allows, allow the children to classify according to their own characteristics first. This can either be done inside using pictures, but it is much better to do it outside with the children finding real creatures so they can see the actual size, colour and how they move.

You can use decision trees, branching trees, Venn diagrams, Carroll diagrams and other types of sorting diagrams (which can be constructed and adapted easily to suit the ability of the children or sourced online) to organise and classify creatures. This obviously links directly to areas of maths, but allows the work to be carried out in a real context.

You can then introduce the fact that mini-beasts can be classified according to the number of legs they have. Children love using the proper, scientific names (molluscs, gastropods, insect, arachnid, crustacean or isopod, myriapod…). Support the children in working out which creature fits into which category and keep a tally of the number of each you can identify so that you can use the data in maths.

I have concentrated here on mini-beasts, but this work can obviously also be carried out with trees and plants, and in doing so will allow the children to have a wider knowledge of the area in which they live. Many fantastic commercial identification charts are available, but it isn't difficult to make your own. The choice between the two may depend on your children: for those who might find this work trickier, having home-made charts that only include the plants, trees or creatures they are going to find is preferable; more able children may rise to the challenge of identifying from a wider range of possibilities.

Environmental change

Learning objective
Recognise that environments can change and that this can sometimes pose dangers to living things.

Cross-curricular links
English, PDL, geography

Soft skills development
Forethought, ability to predict, communication, explanation

Resources
Map of the school grounds/local area, tracing paper, pencil, colouring pencils

What to do
This work is very effective if the children have carried out work on identification and know what lives in their local area, as the children then have ownership and more care for where they live and what difference changes may make.

Having a map of the grounds or local area allows the children to see exactly how things are at the moment. Take the children outside and ask them to identify the different places on the map so they are developing their map skills as well. Place a sheet of tracing paper over the top of the map and suggest that a small estate of, say, three new houses needs to be built somewhere on the site (exactly what needs to be built will obviously depend on the site you are investigating). Challenge the children to work out where the buildings need to be located; what there needs to be other than buildings (roads, parking, gardens, footpaths etc.); why they have selected this location; and what impact it may have on the local environment. All their ideas can be recorded on the tracing paper, which will allow the children to physically see the potential change.

Once the children have done this work and considering the impact it may have on a location they know, you can more easily ask them to consider real planning applications in the local area and the positive and negative impacts they may also have.

Letters can be written to the local council, which allows for explanatory and potentially persuasive writing to take place with a real outcome which, hopefully, would elicit a reply.

Living things and their habitats: Year 5

Describing life cycles

Describe the differences in the life cycles of a mammal, an amphibian, an insect and a bird.

I won't discuss this area of work very much, but if it is possible to have some frog spawn in the classroom or if you can observe some in a pond, then the children will see life cycles at first-hand. The alternatives are hatching chicks (there may be somewhere local where you can borrow and incubate some eggs), or you can buy butterfly hatching kits. All these things are valuable in giving children first-hand experience of life cycles which could otherwise be quite a dull, paper exercise.

Reproductive systems

Learning objective
Describe the life process of reproduction in some plants and animals.

Cross-curricular links
Maths, geography

Soft skills development
Attention to detail, observation, commitment, organisation

Resources
Seeds, pots, compost, outside planting area

What to do
Non-statutory guidance in the National Curriculum talks about studying life cycles and life processes of plants and animals that live in the local environment before then comparing these with plants and animals from around the world.

This would suggest that there needs to be an element of a longitudinal study, with children planting and watching how growth happens over time. Certainly plan ahead and select plants that will germinate during the required period of time.

Ask the children to look closely at the seed/bulb they are starting with. They can make predictions about how it will grow – and the more able children can start to think about why. They can also suggest where the seed has come from. The children will need to be able to record what happens over time. It is important, I think, to plant a range of seeds so that difference can be observed, and the children have more knowledge when they come to making comparisons with plants from other environments.

Living things and their habitats: Year 6

Classifying living things

Learning objective
- Describe how living things are classified into broad groups according to common observable characteristics and based on similarities and differences, including micro-organisms, plants and animals;
- Give reasons for classifying plants and animals based on specific characteristics.

Cross-curricular links
Maths, geography

Soft skills development
Reasoning, thinking, communicating, explaining

Resources
Chalks, pictures and models of creatures and plants from different classifications, examples of real plants from the school grounds and/or local environment

What to do
By the time they get to Year 6, the children should have a really good knowledge of what lives in their grounds, both plants and animals, and they will have had some experience of classifying. In Year 6, it is now possible to introduce the standard classification system – but trying to draw that on the board or on a piece of paper is a challenge for even the neatest amongst us.

Do some research in the classroom first, investigating characteristics of mammals, birds, fish, etc. and challenge the children to list on paper as many plants and animals they can think of in a given time – a list they can then take outside with them.

Then take the learning outside. As long as you have a playground you can create a classification tree large enough for the whole class to use effectively, allowing for conversation and debate.

Create the diagram with the children or prepare it before if you choose, and encourage the children to place both pictures you have provided and the names on their lists in the correct places. Some will be obvious, but others will create some discussion so it might be useful to have an iPad or encyclopaedia with you, and also definitions of the different animal and plant classes so the children can refer back to them.

Research into the development of classification will show when the systems were developed. Since then, things have changed. Be prepared to have conversations with children about not only where certain plants and animals fit, but also about the fact that the traditional classification of humans into men and women isn't actually as clear cut as it used to be. It is worth being prepared for such questions and discussions and knowing how to answer so that it complies with your Sex and Relationships Education (SRE) policy… although you may find that information in relation to transgender and other issues may not be as up-to-date as the children's knowledge.

Living things and their habitats investigations

- Which surfaces do snails like moving on best? (Year 1 and 2)
- Which foods do different mini-beasts like best? (Year 1 and 2)
- Can you build and test a waterproof shelter for a creature living in your school grounds? (Year 3 and 4) (I have done this by giving children a soft toy of a creature that may live in our grounds. They have built structures for them and tested them with water from watering cans. Improvements have been made and testing has continued until either they are perfect, or time has run out!)

Light: Year 3

Shadows

Learning objectives
- Recognise that shadows are formed when the light from a light source is blocked by an opaque object;
- Find patterns in the way that the size of shadows change.

Cross-curricular links
Maths

Soft skills development
Attention to detail, prediction and planning, questioning

Resources
Chalks, metre sticks

What to do
Take a range of materials outside and let the children experiment with trying to make shadows. Make sure you provide a range of transparent, translucent and opaque materials and ask the children to sort them as they test them – then you can introduce the specific vocabulary.

Once the children have tested the items you have provided, let them find their own from around the grounds and test those too. Have discussions about the number of man-made and natural materials that fit into each category. Are there any that there are disagreements about?

Looking at patterns in how shadows change can allow the children to work scientifically. You can simply go outside every hour, have children stand in the same place each time and draw round the shadow created. You can measure the length of each shadow to make it more mathematical and allow graphs to be created. This would also allow you to ask your more able scientists to make predictions about the position and length of shadows.

Light: Year 6

How light travels

Learning objectives
- Recognise that light appears to travel in straight lines;
- Use the idea that light travels in straight lines to explain that objects are seen because they give out or reflect light into the eye;
- Use the idea that light travels in straight lines to explain why shadows have the same shape as the objects that cast them;
- Explain that we see things because light travels from light sources to our eyes or from light sources to objects and then to our eyes.

Cross-curricular links
Maths

Soft skills development
Attention to detail, prediction and planning, questioning, organisation, team work

Resources
Chalk, mirrors, card, sticky tape

What to do
Start by revisiting shadows, using the experience to remind children about the light work they did in Year 3 and start to focus on the fact that light travels in straight lines, which is the focus of the Year 6 work. Ask the children to explain why shadows are formed and why they are the same shape, albeit a different size, as the object creating them. The concept of light travelling in straight lines ought to become apparent, and then you can move on to investigations to explore the phenomena.

If you have areas of the school where there are 'blind corners', it's really interesting to see if the children can position mirrors to help them see round the corners. They don't need to be permanent fixtures, but working together to get the mirrors in the correct position, height and angle can be a real challenge. Groups working in threes with one person each side of the blind corner and another holding a mirror works well. If you have larger groups, the other can record the results, either on the floor or on a map. It is a great way to reinforce the fact that light travels in straight lines and how we see things. It can also inform and support work in angles in maths.

Making periscopes also supports understanding of the objectives, but use your grounds to think of a specific purpose or problem to solve so the reason for making the periscope is a real one. It could be to do with seeing higher up trees without disturbing things that are living there, or you could even set it up as part of a spy challenge... I'll leave that one up to your imagination!

Light investigations

- What are the best materials to make a reflective jacket to make walking to school in the winter safer? Test them outside. (Year 3 and 4)
- Which natural objects make the best shadow puppets? Why? (Year 3 and 4)
- Can you estimate the size of an object from the size of its shadow? If not, what other information do you need to know? (Year 5 and 6)
- If you wanted to leave a trail for someone to follow with a torch, which would be the best stones to use? (Year 5 and 6)

Sound: Year 4

Volume of sounds

Learning objectives
- Find patterns between the volume of a sound and the strength of the vibrations that produced it;
- Recognise that sounds get fainter as the distance from the sound source increases.

Cross-curricular links
English, maths

Soft skills development
Prediction and planning, questioning, organisation, team work, problem solving

Resources
Instruments, bell or whistle

What to do
In this section, I am concentrating on sound and volume, rather than how sound is produced and pitch. Production of sound and vibrations, I think, needs to proceed other work as this is one of the key ideas that other learning and investigations are built on. Pitch can be explored through many methods but will probably include the use of instruments (both manufactured and man-made).

Experimenting volume, by its pure definition, is probably best done outside! Firstly, just sit and listen. Try to recognise not only the different sounds that can be heard, but also where they are coming from. Sitting in the middle of your grounds in silence for a few minutes is a very calming, but also eye-opening experience for some, especially when children spend much time outside rushing around and being busy! Spend a few minutes just listening, and then ask the children to identify what they heard. Discussion can take place about how far away the object is that is making the noise, and how we know.

You could ask the children to close their eyes, and when you hear a sound, say what it is and ask them to point in the direction it is coming from. Share the results with the children when they open their eyes – it can be really interesting and, as not all the children will point in the same direction to identify the source of the noise. This helps the children to realise that sound travels in waves, not straight lines (although it isn't necessary for children to understand this concept).

In order to experiment with the concept that sound gets fainter as you move further from the source, take out a range of instruments with different pitches and, starting close to the source, ask the children to move away from it until they can no longer hear it.

*   Can they hear a triangle or a drum from the furthest distance?
*   Does pitch affect the distance at which we hear sound?
*   How might this not be a fair test?
*   Is it possible to make it a fair test?
*   Can you record the distances and use your findings to support both science and maths work?

A good investigation, using all the key ideas that the children have developed and understood, can centre around ringing the bell or blowing the whistle at the end of playtime. The children could investigate which is the best item to use – whistle, bell, triangle, drum, etc. They could see which produces the sound that travels furthest. An alternative, or supplementary investigation would be to discover where the best place is to stand in the school grounds to signal the end of playtime so that everyone can hear, wherever they are playing. Real-life investigations such as these really do provide a real purpose to investigations – especially if the children can feed it back to the Headteacher, maybe in a report, and the results are acted upon!

Sound investigations

*   Investigate the best material for a string telephone (string, wool, cotton, coated wire…) and test outside. (Year 4)
*   On a sound walk, listen for sounds and then try to identify what was vibrating to make the noise. (Year 4)
*   Should the wearing of woolly hats or hoodies be prohibited when crossing the road to increase safety? (Year 4)

Earth and space: Year 5

The solar system

Learning objectives
- Describe the movement of the Earth and other planets relative to the Sun in the solar system;
- Describe the movement of the Moon relative to the Earth.

Cross-curricular links
English, maths, art

Soft skills development
Perseverance, explaining, questioning, creativity, understanding

Resources
Information cards about planets, string or toilet paper

What to do
I do find work on Earth and Space listed in the National Curriculum quite limiting and as children tend to have a real curiosity for planets and the solar system and if you can find the time, branching out a bit further is a really valuable and inspiring option. It is also true that, if you need to look at the movements of the planets in relation to the sun, knowing about the planets makes this more real.

Start by making fact cards about the planets and the sun (which include both information and photos), hang them round the grounds and ask the children to read and either answer specific questions or retrieve the three facts they find most interesting. Record these in some form (children do tend to love little booklets, but other forms of recording sheets can work too). I have developed this by asking the children to draw the planets on the playground, in chalk, and annotate their drawings. They can be done in the order they are from the sun, which will reinforce any mnemonics you may have taught them to remember the order. Once some knowledge about the planets is acquired, including how long each takes to orbit the sun, you can then make human models of the solar system to show relative movement. It can be quite a challenge – drawing orbit lines on the playground can help the direction of travel, but the timings are always interesting! The children usually work out how to make a best fit and certainly get the idea that planets orbit at different speeds. There are models on the internet that you can use either at the beginning of the process, during, or even at the end so the children can compare their attempts with a computer version.

When considering the orbit of the sun, earth and moon, give the children specific facts and ask them to interpret them in order to make a human model. The facts aren't complicated (the Earth rotates as it orbits the sun, one side of the moon always faces the earth as it orbits...) but putting them into practice takes some grit and determination to get it right! Scale models of the solar system can also be attempted using string to show the relative distances. You probably need to concentrate on either size or distance rather than both, as combining them is difficult, if not impossible, if you want to include all planets.

Evolution and inheritance: Year 6

Although it appears that evolution and inheritance only comes into the Year 6 curriculum, it does lead nicely on from elements of animals and habitats work earlier in key stage 2 (including fossils in Year 3), as well as elements of the key stage 1 science curriculum.

Adaptation and evolution

Learning objective
Identify how animals and plants are adapted to suit their environment in different ways and how that adaptation may lead to evolution.

Cross-curricular links
Art

Soft skills development
Questioning, explaining, hypothesising, listening

Resources
Collecting pots, magnifying glasses, paper, pencils, clipboards

What to do
My practice is: always try to work with concrete examples first and then widen teaching to the more abstract. So, when considering how plants and animals are adapted to their environment, start with the school grounds. Go out and find creatures and plants, investigate their habitat and explain how they are suited and adapted. Think about shape, colour, how they move, eat and drink, protection… Annotated scientific diagrams are a useful way of recording this information.

To start thinking about evolution, suggest to the children what the local environment may be like in 50 or 100 years' time. Consider the impact of global warming and what effect it will have on temperature, rainfall and moisture levels.

- Which current characteristics that the animals have will help them survive as climate changes?
- How will the creatures in your grounds have to evolve in order to continue to survive?
- What will be the consequences if they don't or can't?

Following on from the annotated drawing earlier, children could draw a further one showing and explaining how they will have to change over time. Using an overlay of tracing paper on top of the original drawing will encourage deeper thought when predicting possible adaptations.

Evolution and inheritance investigation

- Compare the characteristics of a cactus to a native plant. Set up an experiment to look after them in exactly the same way. Do they react identically? If there are differences, why? (Year 6)

3 History Outdoors

What does the National Curriculum say?

The National Curriculum states that the purpose of study for history is the following:

A high-quality history education will help pupils gain a coherent knowledge and understanding of Britain's past and that of the wider world. It should inspire pupils' curiosity to know more about the past. Teaching should equip pupils to ask perceptive questions, think critically, weigh evidence, sift arguments, and develop perspective and judgement. History helps pupils to understand the complexity of people's lives, the process of change, the diversity of societies and relationships between different groups, as well as their own identity and the challenges of their time.

Outdoor learning in history undoubtedly inspires pupil's curiosity. Planning quality learning experiences outside encourages children to 'ask perceptive questions, think critically, weigh evidence, sift arguments and develop perspective and judgement'. Learning through practical opportunities outside allows pupils to develop an understanding of 'people's lives' in different eras, and encourages them to see 'the process of change'. I would suggest that a high-quality history education needs to include aspects of outdoor learning.

As a result, the learning opportunities suggested in this section will inform and enhance history learning and experiences. It will be more powerful if seen as part of a progression of lessons, rather than stand-alone sessions, so please do consider how they will dovetail into your plans, or how your plans can be adapted to include some or all of the experiences suggested.

This section starts with a two generic ideas that can be adapted to most historical periods of study. They also benefit from being repeated – across all year groups as they can be developed and adapted depending on the age, ability and independence of the children you are working with. Following this, there are sections which address each period of history that has to be studied during the primary phase.

These activities are suitable for all ages within both key stages, and can be easily adapted to suit the topic and the ability of the children you are working with.

Timelines

Cross-curricular links
English, maths, art

Soft skills development
Team work, negotiation, planning, accuracy

Resources
Chalks, metre sticks, date labels relevant to the time period investigating

Creating timelines on the playground promotes great chronological understanding

What to do
Talk to the children about what the term 'chronology' means and relate it to their own experiences, if necessary. Perhaps also give the children a pack of dates in a small group to put in chronological order before going outside. This way they will get used to the dates and information and can discuss the content before applying it to the timeline.

Outside, the children will need to work in groups to construct a timeline relevant to the dates you are working within. You can either guide them by modelling, for example, that one metre represents 100 years, or you could ask the children to work out the scale for themselves, perhaps by measuring the space they have first. With younger children, you could prepare the timelines yourself.

Having drawn the timeline and put the dates on, you could play a game, asking the children to stand on specific dates to make sure they understand how the dates work. For example, give the children a date and ask them to find where that would be on the timeline. This can be differentiated according to the children's ability – those that need to be challenged can be given, say 483AD, and others could have 450AD. You could also do some work on rounding to the closest hundred. Give the children date cards again and ask them to go to the hundred that is closest to their date.

Once the children are comfortable with the timelines, they can use a pack of information cards with dates (which can be custom made or adapted from resources readily available from a quick Google search online) to either place in the correct place on the timeline, or they can summarise the information and write it on the playground in the correct place. They could, alternatively, create an image to represent what happened.

Having carried out this activity on a number of occasions, I am absolutely convinced I would always do timelines outside before doing them on a piece of paper, if at all. Working outside allows the children to work on a scale which means that they develop a much better understanding of how long time actually is… some of my quicker workers have actually managed to extend their timelines from the Romans to the current day, and take it back to Greek times giving them and the rest of the class a real 'awe and wonder' moment!

Fact finding

Cross-curricular links
English

Soft skills development
Team work, developing memory skills, co-operation

Resources
Information cards, pencils, recording booklets, clipboards

What to do
It is often useful at the beginning of a topic for you to know that the children in your class have a shared knowledge of the subject you are studying. This approach is helpful across a range of topics, with all year groups and with work differentiated for different ages and abilities.

Create a set of fact cards. You could even create two sets with differing amounts of information and have the one with more detail mounted on a different coloured piece of paper so the children know the difference. Laminate the cards (for future use) and hang them up around the school grounds.

Give the children a booklet or an alternative recording sheet in which to record the information from the cards (it's lovely to get them to do the front cover while you're doing the register if appropriate). Have a base outside where the children leave their booklets, clipboards and pencils. The idea is they go, in groups of two or three, to find a card, read it in their head and aloud to a partner, and listen to them read it aloud too. Then they have to return to base and record the main elements in their booklets. Having the children return to base also means you, as the teacher, can keep an eye on them to see what they are doing and how efficient they are being – they are not just disappearing into the school grounds for half an hour at a time! If time is running short and the work hasn't been completed, collect the cards in for the last ten minutes and allow the children to fill in any missing gaps, ensuring they do all have the information they need to know.

There are times when it's appropriate to let the children take clipboards with them so they're not expected to rely on their memory. I still encourage reading the texts to each other but this makes the information retrieval a bit quicker and potentially more accurate.

I always make sure I have an extension, reinforcement activity which allows me to see how much the children have retained and understood. This could be the children taking it in turns to be quiz master and contestant to test how much they have understood and retained. Or I sometimes take topic books outside so once the children have finished the quiz, they can research more about one or two of the concepts they have started to learn about.

I am explicit with the children about them developing memory and that reading, speaking and listening are three methods that can help. I relate this to things like learning spellings and times tables. I also show them pictures of a brain which suggests that physical activity can help stimulate mental activity, which is really powerful.

Key stage 1

As the themes for key stage 1 history give many options for choice and can be dependent on your locality, the ideas listed here will be quite general, allowing them to be adapted to different topics and situations. The fact finding and timeline activities can also be easily adapted to suit key stage 1 children and topics.

Changes within living memory

This topic is so vague and open to interpretation in many ways that offering suggestions is difficult. But I have made the assumption that schools might use this topic to allow the children to investigate themselves and their families.

Cross-curricular links
English, science, maths, PDL

Soft skills development
Creativity, explaining and reasoning, observation

Resources
Chalks, metre sticks, tape measures, fruit and veg

What to do
If this topic investigates how the children have grown, draw around them in chalk and measure. Ask them to then draw what they think their size was two years ago, and then earlier again. This gives a good mix of history and maths and also links to science. Predictions can obviously be made about how big they will be when they are older.

If you have a growing area in your grounds, look at how what the children eats changes over time. Pick some vegetables, puree some and have some whole. Try them and discuss why food is prepared differently for different ages.

Draw number lines on the playground and ask the children to write the names of their families in the right place according to ages. It could then be developed into some mental maths. For example, you could ask the children to say how old people would be in 10 years time, or how old they were 10 years before. Could the children work out combined ages? The possibilities are numerous.

Beyond living memory

Learning objectives
Events beyond living memory that are significant nationally or globally and the lives of significant individuals in the past.

I have combined these two learning objectives as they are often dealt with together in schools, and the ideas for outdoor learning can be used for both aspects.

Cross-curricular links
English, science, maths

Soft skills development
Creativity, explaining and reasoning, observation, questioning, planning

Resources
Role play cards, dressing up clothes, chalks

What to do
Role playing different situations in the school grounds always brings history to life for children. Hot seating, what happens next, dressing up and assuming different roles are all valuable, and a lot easier in terms of space and noise if they can be done outside rather than in the classroom. Children can use a variety of props either from inside or from the grounds and the range of different settings can also help the imagination.

Drawing maps on the playground can really help to illustrate events of both national and global significance. Being able to physically move from one place to another gives the children a better feeling for and understanding of location that can't be achieved from just looking at maps. You can either draw the maps yourself, get the children to have a go, or do half and half (you draw the outline and ask the children to add the details). Maps can obviously be of countries and continents, or of towns and villages, depending on the topic being studied. LEGO®, boxes and other resources can be used to enhance the work as appropriate.

Significant historical events, people and places in their own locality

This area of study is so obviously location specific that the ideas are very general. We have a steam train line in Alton, and had a battle in the Civil War in town, so both those aspects would lead to some great outdoor learning (including getting local historians in to help re-create a battle scene on the field!). When thinking about the historical study of your local area, do be as creative as you can in terms of outdoor learning. Food, treasure hunts, creating pictures, role play, chalks and more can be used to enhance and enrich your class's learning experiences.

Cross-curricular links
English, science, maths

Soft skills development
Questioning, attention to detail, observation

Resources
Photos of local area, historical information cards, log books

What to do
Investigating what can be seen from the school grounds is an interesting exercise. You could give the children photos of different views and ask them to identify them. It is also possible to age buildings by giving the children relevant sketches of brickwork or roof patterns from different periods in history, and asking them to identify these patterns in various buildings. The school building itself may also give clues to the past and might be worth investigating. Old, new, or a mixture of both, architecture can be considered, as well as the previous use of the building or its land. Log books will give information about the history of the school.

In our school, inviting people from the local community is classed as outside learning. Within every community, there are numerous people who have a wealth of information about local history, and there will almost certainly be someone who is willing and able to talk to your class.

Although this book concentrates on learning within the school grounds, it is important to mention at this point that walks around your local area are crucial. From leaving the gate, give children things to look for, note down, remember and tell their adult so they are consistently and constantly involved in enquiry – even if are heading to a specific place, the walk there and back can be full of learning opportunities.

Key stage 2

In my experience, and due to the chronological nature of the history curriculum, the Stone Age is often studied in Year 3, alongside studies of rocks and soils (science). This is certainly what happens at Anstey and we find the two areas mutually supportive. If this is the case in your school, do look at the rocks and soils part of the science chapter in this book and see how the ideas reinforce each other.

Changes in Britain from the Stone Age to the Iron Age: Key stage 2

Sorting flints

Cross-curricular links
English

Soft skills development
Problem solving, explaining and reasoning, listening, discussing

Resources
A range of flints, paintbrushes, cloths and water, labels

What to do
Ideally, if you have time, bury the flints in a specific area of the school grounds prior to the lesson, then the children will be excavating as well as sorting. Discuss with the children that flints were used as a main tool for a variety of different purposes during the Stone Age. Hand around a selection of flints so that the children can suggest the reasons why they were useful – hardness and shape, as well as its availability. Introduce labels saying what these purposes were to ensure development of vocabulary (gouging, cutting, scraping...).

Outside, explain to the children that they are going to be archaeologists. They will have to search for flints (identify them from other types of rock and stone), clean them, and sort them using the labels to put them into piles. The children will also have to explain their thinking and be able to persuade others in their group during the sorting.

Following on from this activity, it is possible to write reports, do presentations, take measurements, do some observational drawings, or carry out some scientific testing of the flints to see whether they do the jobs suggested.

Fossils

Cross-curricular links
Science

Soft skills development
Creativity, explaining and
reasoning, observation

Resources
Booklets, playdough or
plasticine, crayons, pencils, real
fossils and pictures of fossils,
video about different types of
fossils

What to do
Start the session by having
a range of photos of fossils

Making rubbings of 'fossils of the future'

and real fossils on tables. Many children will have some knowledge of what they are, and
allowing them to move around the tables, look, feel and discuss will allow them to share their
knowledge and experiences. It will also allow you as the teacher to share in this, recognise prior
knowledge, and use it during the rest of the lesson.

Use a video to show how fossils are formed and what different types of fossils there are. There
are a number available which simply and clearly underline the fact that fossils are made from
living things, and their formation started millions of years ago. Having watched the video, the
children might be able to categorise the fossils that are on their tables.

Going outside, the children each have a recording booklet, a pencil, a crayon and a piece of
plasticine or playdough. I challenge them to try to discover objects in our grounds which may
become the fossils of the future, remembering that fossils were once living things. They can
make prints using playdough, make rubbings in their books using crayons or draw what they see,
making sure images are labelled. These experiences will give an impression of what the objects
might look like were they to become fossils.

Cave painting

Cross-curricular links
Science, art

Soft skills development
Creativity, questioning, observation

Resources
Paint trays, paint brushes, water, paper

What to do
This activity can be done on many different levels, depending on how authentic you want to be and how much time you have. It is possible to carry out the

Cave painting using paints made from natural resources

whole process using purely natural resources, or you can include some modern equivalents if you wish.

As a minimum, get the children to make their own paints. This can be done by using a range of soils and rocks (soil from the grounds, clay, compost, limestone) and different fruits and berries (either scavenged or bought). Mixing or crushing the resources in a pallet or pot with a little water makes a really effective natural paint. You can use a stick to mix which will add to the authenticity.

Instead of using plastic pots, you could try to find natural alternatives. Some children decided to use a piece of bark to mix on, others some slate, others did the mixing directly on the path.

It is also possible to make paint brushes by using a stick and vegetation: tie straw or thicker grass, grasses or other vegetation onto the end of a stick. Children love to do this and it does teach them a bit of resilience, as it doesn't tend to work the first time and can fall to pieces. But if you want a more genuine historical experience, it is certainly worth a go!

Obviously precede painting with the children researching and investigating examples of real cave paintings. Once ready and with whichever type of paint brush you choose to use, paintings can be done on small bits of paper, long rolls to make a collaborative piece, or even straight onto a floor or wall if you have one that is appropriate.

Neolithic stone balls

Cross-curricular links
English, art, PDL

Soft skills development
Creativity, questioning, observation, debating and reasoning

Resources
Images of stone balls, clay (naturally sourced or commercially bought)

What to do
Investigating areas of history where no-one actually knows what the answers are is perfect in helping children to take on the role of a real historian. Neolithic stone balls from the Stone Age have been found in their hundreds but no-one is really sure what they might have been used for.

The historical part of this session is asking children to investigate the stone balls, what archaeologists think they were used for, analysing their arguments and coming up with their own theories based on evidence. This process can be entirely oral or finish with a piece of written argument. This can be done in the classroom, or equally well outside where noise levels aren't as important and children can move around freely to look at different stimuli and talk to other peers.

I think it seems obvious to follow this level of investigation with some creative work. Children can try to recreate some of the patterns from the balls using sketch books – but it is even better if they can follow this up by using a stick to draw patterns into wettish soil. This would help them to understand much better how natural materials aren't as predictable as pencil and paper. Having rehearsed patterns, children can then be taught to make spheres of clay – solid or using two coil pots – add the five or six 'knobs' on the side and decorate. A few years ago I had a potter friend work with children in school – she recommended doing clay work outside as often as possible. There is more space, the children don't have to be as careful with handprints on walls or furniture, and they are often less distracted by others and concentrate more outside. And, when clay work is being done as a response to a history stimulus, you are creating a more authentic environment.

If you don't have a kiln, a friendly secondary school might fire them for you, or you could have a camp and fire them yourselves. Alternatively, use the self-hardening clay that is now available.

The Roman Empire and its impact on Britain: Key stage 2

The Roman Empire is a fantastic and exciting area of study. The Roman invasion and settlement in Britain means that across the country there are places to visit that can bring the topic to life. These visits can be supported by a range of outdoor learning activities that can take place within your own school grounds.

Roman mosaic pictures

Cross-curricular links
Art

Soft skills development
Team work, negotiation, communication, creativity, resilience, attention to detail

Resources
Pictures of mosaics, natural resources, PowerPoint of examples of land art

What to do
One approach is to stimulate discussion in the classroom by using pictures of mosaics which are on tables or an interactive

Pictures made from natural resources based on Roman mosaics – just beautiful!

whiteboard. Children have a chance to wander and look at them all, before talking about what they are, when they are from, what they were used for, what they were made of, any common features etc. Following on from this, explain to the class that they are going to try to replicate the images using natural resources found in the grounds. At this point, some images of land art which illustrate, for example, use of colour, different resources and shape is really inspiring. Then the children, working in small groups, can select an image and attempt to recreate it in the grounds. It is great to do this in autumn when there are a wide range of leaf colours and berries that can be used, but it is effective at any time of the year.

If you are short of resources in your grounds, it is possible to ask the children to bring some in with them, go collecting yourself, or put a note up for other staff requesting the same (most staff are more than happy to help if they can, especially those who walk dogs!).

It is worth mentioning that you need to make sure that all the materials that are accessible to the children to use are safe. Do have a good look round your grounds and make sure you have checked there is nothing that could harm, and do cross-reference this with any allergies the children may have. Even having taken these steps, do make sure children wash their hands when they have finished the activity and tell them not to put fingers in mouths! You could take some bottles of hand cleaner out with you and give everyone a 'squirt' immediately as you finish.

Roman mosaic patterns

Cross-curricular links
Art, maths, English

Soft skills development
Team work, negotiation, communication, creativity, resilience, attention to detail, ability to give and take advice

Resources
Pictures of mosaic patterns, chalks, rulers and/or metre sticks

What to do
This builds on beautifully from the work on mosaic pictures in the sense that the children already have background

Creating Roman patterns requires patience and resilience

knowledge and have experimented with the creative side of mosaics. This activity needs them to be more precise and children need to be willing to try, try and try again!

Show the children images of mosaics, but draw their attention to the repeated patterns that frame many of the pictures. Explain that the task is to try to recreate these patterns – using chalks on the playground. Explain as well that the task will require a lot of redrafting as they will be required to evaluate each other's work and offer suggestions for improvement. You may even need to model how these suggestions can be made so they sound encouraging and positive, and how they can be received and acted upon!

A brilliant example of how effective this can be is Austin's Butterfly (see Bibliography for link). It illustrates a young boy making six improvements to his picture of a butterfly based on peer feedback, and can be used with children to show the effectiveness of this approach. It is worth noting that John Hattie found that feedback is one of the most important factors in ensuring progress in learning.

When the children go outside, make sure they have a pattern and access to chalks and let them start. Have rulers or metre sticks and let children use them as appropriate as the session progresses. You could demonstrate how to measure and mark to make guidelines to ensure repeated patterns are all the same size. It might be worth writing number 1 next to their first attempt, then 2 and so on, so they and others can see improvements. Either have regular set intervals when improvement suggestions are made, or encourage the children to ask for advice at the right time.

At the end of the session, celebrate both the outcomes and the process – and it might also be worth drawing comparisons with redrafting writing and work in other curriculum areas.

Roman marching

Cross-curricular links
History, maths, geography

Soft skills development
Team work, negotiation, communication, resilience

Resources
Chalks, metre sticks, maps of Roman roads, lengths of Roman roads

What to do
Ask the children to mark out a starting and finishing line 10 metres apart. It is useful if they are all alongside each other so the groups don't end up marching into each other's spaces! Challenge the class, in groups of three, four or five to march in perfect time for 10 metres. How can they start and finish together, always starting on the same leg? How can they regulate their stride lengths so they are always the same? What are they going to do with their arms? This may take quite a while!

Once they have achieved perfection (and you will know what that looks like for your children!), ask them to count how many steps it takes to cover 10 metres. So how many steps for 100 metres, and one km? Can they work out how many steps it would take to walk along some of the Roman roads? All calculations can be done in chalks on the playground.

There are different elements to this task so different children will excel in different areas within one lesson.

Building bridges

Cross-curricular links
DT, science, maths

Soft skills development
Resilience, determination, using initiative, planning, co-operation

Resources
Willow (or other flexible wood), harder sticks, string, water, weights

What to do
Start in the classroom having a look at photos of viaducts and aquaducts. Discuss what they are, when they date from, what they were made from, and what makes

Building successful bridges using problem solving and teamwork

them strong enough to have lasted as long as they have (the arches – and the Romans were the first to use arches in buildings).

Outside, have lengths of willow, or similar, ready to be cut and used. Challenge the children to create a line of willow arches, all the same size, similar to the ones they saw in the pictures of viaducts. This is harder than it looks and they will need to think about how to stop the ends of the willow pinging back out of the ground!

Once this has been achieved, another parallel row can be made (quite quickly) and the sticks placed across so you have an actual 'bridge'. At this point, weights can be put on to see how much it will hold. It is useful to let the children know that at some point their construction will collapse (to avoid huge disappointment!), but if they look where it collapses then they can rebuild it even stronger.

An extension for this is to look at other bridge designs and discuss where they get their strength from. Triangles are obviously extremely useful and further structures can be made using non-flexible wood that can also be tested.

Nine Men's Morris

Cross-curricular links
English, maths

Soft skills development
Team work, strategy, communication, attention to detail, problem solving, ability to win and lose

Resources
Instruction cards, chalks

What to do
Nine Men's Morris is a game that was invented by the Romans (you can find instructions for the game on my website: www. outsidelearning.co.uk). Initial

Developing history, maths and English skills through playing Nine Men's Morris

discussion, related to excavations and primary sources of evidence, can centre around how we know this. It is also interesting to discuss, in relation to the game, how much we know for certain and how much is a modern interpretation. For example, the board has been found as well as nine counters for each player, so we can be as certain as possible that this information is historical fact. Whether the rules were also found, or whether these have been developed since, I'm not sure but it does create some really interesting historical discussion.

It's worth going through the instructions and rules if you think your class will need a bit of support. Outside, this game works best if the children play against each other in pairs, as this can promote better discussion and development of strategy. The children draw the board on the playground (this may take a few goes!) and then they need to find nine counters each (stones, twigs, leaves...) and play the game. It is worth having a 'dummy run' first so everyone is happy with the rules, and then play a few games, swapping partners if desired.

At the end of one session, one of my children asked what would happen if there were four concentric squares instead of three, or if the board was triangular instead of square? So the next session spend time letting the children design their own versions of the game, adjusting the style of the board and number of counters needed – an amazing problem solving exercise which also developed resilience. Some will take ages to find a successful formula and some won't even manage, but the process will still make the exercise worthwhile.

The other benefit of this activity is that it has a positive, knock-on impact at playtimes. Other children see the boards on the playground, ask what the rules are and then spend their time happily playing.

The Anglo-Saxons, Scots and Vikings: Key stage 2

I have grouped all these periods of history together as there is obvious flow and overlap between them. I think geography may have an influence on the amount of time different schools spend on elements of this historical period: certain places in Britain have more historical relevance to different areas of the country, leading to potential off-site visits which enhance learning opportunities. For example, if you are near York, the opportunities to learn about the Vikings are powerful and relevant, whereas schools located in Winchester may find they prioritise the Anglo-Saxons. Wherever you are though, and however you plan your curriculum, the following activities will support children's learning and understanding of lives during this historical period.

Making natural dyes

Cross-curricular links
English, science, maths, art

Soft skills development
Problem solving, team work, using initiative, creativity

Resources
Pots, measuring jugs, water, fabric swatches (old sheets or pillow cases cut up), berries and fruits

What to do
People from all these periods of history used natural dyes on their clothes. Children love experimenting and, as with many outdoor activities, you can give your class as much or as little freedom as they are ready for and you feel comfortable with. You can either make the resources available, present some guidelines and let them get on; or you can be prescriptive and guide the children more.

Using a variety of materials and resources to make natural dyes

The time of year you are doing this activity will dictate what natural resources are available and what has to be supplied. Beetroot, grass, soil, blueberries and other berries have all been used successfully. The traditional way is to pound them and added water to make a liquid dye – deciding how much water to put in is interesting, and it's worth keeping a check of measurements so the procedure is repeatable. Fabric can then be put in the dye – the children can predict and time how long to leave it for. It can be tie-dyed if you wish, or the children can experiment with achieving different patterns (dip dying, or patterns can be created by drying the fabric over different surfaces like gravel, or textured benches for example). Children can mash the berries and apply straight on to the fabric. This allows for a much stronger colour and gives children the chance to be precise about where colour is added. Leaves can also be used as stencils – place the leaf on the fabric and apply the dye around it.

The options for creating dyed fabric swatches are numerous, but it is always a good idea to make the dyed fabric for a specific purpose to give a purpose to the outcome and process. Perhaps use the finished product to make a topic book cover, or use a swatch to design an outfit for a Saxon person.

Wattle and daub

This can be split into two separate sessions, making the wattle fences in one session, and the daub in the next.

Cross-curricular links
Science, maths, DT

Soft skills development
Problem solving, team work, using initiative, turn taking, communication

Resources
Hazel posts (or similar), willow off-cuts (or similar), water, a range of containers, sand, soil, straw or grass cuttings

What to do
We are lucky in school to have access to hazel and willow, but if you haven't there may well be parents, tree surgeons, the town council or others

Children love experimenting with how to make the best daub to stick to a wattle hurdle

who you may be able to ask – it is worth the effort! However, if you are unable to source the wood for the wattle, you can still have great fun making the daub!

Ask the children to investigate structures from this period of history and they will discover that walls for houses and more were often built using wattle and daub. Through research they will soon rejoice in what went into the daub (straw, water and horse poo!). At this stage it might be worth making it clear that we can experiment with making daub without one certain key ingredient.

There is a great video online of Tony Robinson making daub and applying it to wattle which is worth sharing with the children prior to them getting their hands dirty.

Let the children work in groups to experiment with making daub. Have buckets containing sand, soil, straw/grass cuttings and water and get the children to work in groups to combine different quantities of each to make the best daub they can. To make it more scientific (and this does link directly to mixtures in science) ask the children to plan how they will test which is the best, and what they will use to measure the results. The only parts that really need to be recorded are the quantities of ingredients in each mixture, the results (which could be photographs) and conclusions.

If you have the required wood, work out as a group how far apart to sink the hazel posts into the ground, and in what shape (line, circle…) so that the flexible willow branches can be woven between them. Take it in turns so that all can have a go, and then you can apply the daub for an authentic finish.

One of my children suggested after doing this and dying fabric that she wished she was a Celt as 'stuff like this is so much better than the PlayStation!'.

Making herbal teas

Cross-curricular links
Science, DT (food)

Soft skills development
Team work, creativity, turn taking, communication

Resources
A range of different herbs, pots, warm water, spoons

What to do
During these periods in history, herbs were used extensively in cooking and other areas of life and if you are lucky enough to have a kitchen or a space to make fires, very simple breads can be made with flours, water and herbs or garlic.

Using herbs in cooking and drinks is a firm favourite!

But if this is not possible, herbal teas are also great to experiment with.

Initially, give the children the chance to look at, smell, taste and identify herbs. Try some herb breads or scones to see if they can pick out the flavours. Once the children have formed opinions they can then start to combine (washed) herbs with some warm water (thermos flasks or mugs are useful for this – many schools have them for staff on playground duty). Squashing the herbs before adding the water and then mixing will help to bring out the flavours. Children can taste to see which they like the best (if they each have a straw it makes it hygienic). They can even go on to produce packaging and invent a name.

It is also worth showing them, at some stage in the process, the range of herbal teas available today and appreciate that this is a legacy from times past.

Creating a Celtic/Viking village

Cross-curricular links
DT, English

Soft skills development
Team work, creativity, communication, interpreting information, asking questions

Resources
Information card, LEGO®, chalks, natural resources

What to do
We have evidence from archaeological excavations about what villages from these periods of history were like. Asking the children to interpret this information in a creative manner is really interesting and promotes higher order thinking, explaining and justifying skills – and can pose more questions than answers!

Make an information card with between six and 10 pieces of information that we know about how villages were organised during the relevant period in history. The children can discuss these ideas and start to think about what the village might actually look like on the ground. Let them know that they are going to recreate the village on the playground using chalks, LEGO® and any other resources they like. They have to absolutely stick to the concrete evidence that you have given them but can interpret it in they own way, as long as they can justify and explain their thinking. Exploring the concepts of fact and interpretation is a useful historical process that allows children to see that not all of history is an absolute.

The outcomes of this work can be fantastic – you will know your class but it's worth giving yourselves a bit more time than you think you need! It is amazing how you are likely to get something very different from each group – and this is certainly worth investigating and celebrating at the end of the session.

The achievements of the earliest civilizations: Key stage 2

An overview of where and when the first civilizations appeared and a depth study of one of the following: Ancient Sumer, the Indus Valley, Ancient Egypt, the Shang dynasty of Ancient China

Informal research has suggested to me that the most popular earliest civilization that is studied in school is Ancient Egypt. As such, this section will focus on outdoor learning for this period in history. In relation to Egypt, do also look in the Geography section for work on rivers. This ties in beautifully with work on the River Nile.

Making shadufs

Cross-curricular links
DT, English, maths

Soft skills development
Team work, communication, interpreting information, asking questions, problem solving, resilience, using initiative

Resources
Spaghetti, playdough, sticks, string

What to do
Shadufs were the water lifting machines that Egyptians used to draw water out of the River Nile. I have seen examples of these being made out of dowelling in the classroom, but it is a lot more authentic to take the children outside.

Shadufs can be made to any scale, depending on the availability of sticks

Initially though, it is worth experimenting inside, which is where the spaghetti and playdough (or marshmallows if you're brave!) are useful. Having shown the children pictures of shadufs, ask them to experiment with the materials on offer to make a structure that stands up and has an 'arm' that tips backwards and forwards.

Once this has been done, the children can work outside to make a shaduf using sticks. The size is up to you – coppiced lengths of wood a couple of metres long that the children use for den building can be used. You can also use some that are arm-length or even shorter and the children will still enjoy the process and should get pleasing results.

You may have to teach some knot tying before the children start, and give them time to practice. However, as long as the preparatory work has been done with spaghetti (or similar) the children do tend to work very independently, industriously and with confidence.

Investigating flood plains

Cross-curricular links
English, geography, maths

Soft skills development
Questioning skills, hypothesising, planning, predicting

Resources
Water, variety of water containers, LEGO®, (river vocabulary cards if you want to make the geography link), a slope

What to do
The River Nile was central to Egyptian existence. It is useful to explore its importance and the Egyptians relationship with the river before embarking on practical work.

Once you are outside, work in an area of the school grounds where there is a slope (either grass or concrete will work). Ask each group to identify where the source is going to be and this is where they will always tip their water. Predict what will happen to the water and then tip a cup of water at a time and watch the path it takes. Once enough water has flowed, ask the children to place LEGO® houses in the best places for the Egyptians to live based on their research (close enough to use the water, to be able to grow crops but far enough away so they are not in danger of flooding). Having built houses, retest by making more water flow.

Once the children are happy with the placements of houses, tell them it is the rainy season and increase the water flow by two or three times. See what effect that has on where the water goes – it will indicate where the flood plain is – and see what impact this has on the placement of the houses (some might now be underwater!).

This activity is repeated in the geography (rivers) section as it is obviously also relevant there. However, I make no apologies for listing the idea twice – it is such a fantastic learning experience I don't think the children would mind doing it twice, from different perspectives.

Making paper

Cross-curricular links
English, science, maths

Soft skills development
Team work, delegation, following instructions, attention to detail

Resources
Newspaper, different sorts of papers, leaves, water, glue, pots, paint brushes, netting, plastic sheeting or bags

What to do
It is possible to buy commercial kits to make paper, but the Egyptians wouldn't have had those to make papyrus, so you can have a go without.

Investigate how the Egyptians made paper from papyrus (crushing and flattening papyrus stalks and then laying them at 90° to each other and leaving them to dry – I'm assuming they were sticky so stuck together). Egyptians used papyrus as it is what they had available – so if we are to make our own paper, we also need to use what is available.

In the absence of papyrus, make up a solution of PVA glue and water, and then using a selection of torn papers, crushed leaves, grasses and anything else you want to experiment with, layer the materials with each layer being placed at right angles with glue in between. Care and attention to detail will obviously produce more pleasing results. Paper can be made on the grass, onto netting, plastic sheeting or bags so it can then be moved to a safe place to dry (if you use plastic, do make sure you turn the paper so it will dry on both sides).

Why outside? Firstly, because the children can then have their pick of natural resources to use in the paper you produce. And secondly, because you really don't want to clear up the classroom after this activity! The children can still be careful and respectful of the resources they are using when they are outside, but dribbles of glue on grass are easier to ignore than when they are on the carpet!

Ancient Greece: Key stage 2

A study of Greek life and achievements and their influence on the Western World.

One of the really interesting elements of Greek history is the legacy it has left on modern day life. From democracy to free time activities, from the Olympic Games to language, our life has many links to Ancient Greece. These can be exploited in many ways using outside spaces, enriching and enhancing learning experiences and other curriculum areas.

Democracy

Cross-curricular links
English, PDL

Soft skills development
Empathy, team work, communication

Resources
Role play cards

What to do
This is a drama activity based on democracy in Ancient Greek times. Explore the democratic system with your class and discover who was allowed to vote and who wasn't. Create some role play cards where all members of the class are given the role of a person from Ancient Greek times (young girl, slave, man from the city, man from outside the city etc.). It is useful if the cards also include whether the person is allowed to vote or not, and why.

Encourage the children to then act out scenes from daily life in Ancient Greece, until, say, a bell rings and those who are allowed to, debate and vote. Those who are ineligible to vote listen to the debate (in silence) and wait to see the outcome.

After a couple of rounds of this, have a class discussion to see what people think about the decisions that were made, and the fairness of the process.

We developed this further by looking at our democratic system (as part of PDL and British Values) and inviting our local MP to come and talk to the year group about his experiences in the House of Commons.

Ancient Greek games

Cross-curricular links
PE, maths

Soft skills development
Team work, communication, turn taking, delegation, perseverance

Resources
Sticks, small balls, chalk, hoops, marbles, metre sticks, stop watches, instruction cards (where necessary)

What to do
A variety of games we use today were invented in Greek times. Set up a circuit of any number of the following games and, if you wish, give the children recording sheets to note down distances and times. This adds a slightly competitive streak to the work, in addition to asking the children to use different skills. It is especially useful if you want to use the data for statistics in maths. For example, if children take measurements for the standing long jump, they can then present them as graphs, find the mean and range.

Developing skills and setting challenges 'Greek style'!

Game and activity ideas:
- hockey with sticks and small balls (set up a slalom trail)
- sticks and hoops (also popular in the Victorian times)
- marbles (rolling into a target like an archery board)
- standing jump
- hopscotch
- draughts.

Before or after playing, children can research how these fitted into Greek life (for example, I understand that hopscotch was used as fitness training for the Greek Army). And, as mentioned, a lot of data can be collected to be used in maths, so there are many possibilities to extend and develop these ideas into other curriculum areas.

The Olympic Games

Cross-curricular links
PE, maths

Soft skills development
Team work, communication, turn taking, delegation, perseverance

Resources
Dependant on the activities but mostly equipment you will have in your PE store

What to do
I shall keep this section short as it is something that is easy to combine with your PE lessons.

However, to make it a more meaningful historical exercise, as well as a fun PE lesson, ask the children to research events from the ancient games and compare them with the modern games. Ask why there have been such changes over the years and perhaps even predict what may happen in the future. You could talk to children about the Paralympics, for example.

Once they have a bank of knowledge developed through research and historical enquiry, the children can then develop plans for their own class or school Olympics. They can select a range of events from both ancient and modern times that can be carried out successfully within your grounds. Whether it stays as a class event or you run it for other classes (and even parents!) will depend on time and logistics.

Drawing mazes

Cross-curricular links
English, maths

Soft skills development
Team work, following instructions, communication, resilience

Resources
Some mazes for the children to complete, dotted paper, pencils, chalk, instructions for drawing a maze

Learning to draw mazes is a challenge, but worth the effort!

What to do
This is a great activity which links well to drama lessons covering Theseus and the Minotaur. An initial word of warning – don't assume that all children had done mazes before… many haven't! It is worth starting with mazes on tables in the classroom, so they can all experience completing a maze that has already been drawn before starting to make their own.

Drawing mazes first on dotted paper is the easiest way to start. Find a set of instructions by googling 'Draw your own maze'. There are a large number of options that you can pick from, but I would recommend adapting them to suit you and your class – it might take a little time, but it will be worth the effort. I start by giving each pair a set of instructions and working through together on the interactive white board, asking the children to follow, and come and help construct the maze. In pairs or threes, they can have a go at following the instructions and creating a maze on dotted paper (this can be done inside or outside).

Once outside, challenge the children to convert their paper, small-scale maze into a life size one on the playground. This is often tricky as scaling things up is quite a sophisticated art. Asking the children to think about how they are going to start is always a good idea, so they have a plan of attack before committing chalk to playground. Do let them know it may take two or three goes before they are successful. Having water and cloths available may be useful, so if they make a minor mistake, it can be washed away and there's no need to start all over again!

These mazes also have a great knock-on effect at playtimes where you get lots of other children trying to solve them!

Non-European city: Key stage 2

A non-European society that provides contrasts with British history – one study chosen from: early Islamic civilization, including a study of Baghdad c. AD 900; Mayan civilization c. AD 900; Benin (West Africa) c. AD 900-1300.

There are three choices in this section. At Anstey, we look at early Islamic civilisations, which provide great opportunities for outdoor learning. As such, many of the ideas here fit into this category, but will be adaptable to other contrasting non-European societies.

Islamic patterns

Cross-curricular links
Art, maths

Soft skills development
Team work, creativity, resilience, attention to detail

Resources
Images of Islamic patterns, natural materials

What to do
Islamic tiles and patterns tend to be very geometric, based on symmetry and tessellation. They are beautiful to work on with a more traditional artistic approach drawing and painting, and developing into printing and collage.

Creating images from nature based on Islamic patterns – just beautiful!

However, taking children outside and working with natural resources can produce some amazing pieces of artwork. Share images of Islamic art and show the children some examples of land art by people such as Andy Goldsworthy and Tim Pugh. These will illustrate to the children how colours, shapes and textures from nature can be combined to create beautiful images. It is also worth emphasising that placement of materials, in addition to colour, shape and texture is also important.

When working outside, the children need to create their own Islamic pattern basing their work on an image of an Islamic tile, considering elements of design, tessellation and symmetry. Ask them to critically evaluate their own and others' work both during the process and at the end to ensure the best outcome possible. Take photos to preserve the work, and allow them to evaluate and/or use in further work if required.

Creating Baghdad

Cross-curricular links
English, DT

Soft skills development
Team work, creativity, communication, interpreting information, asking questions

Resources
Information card, LEGO®, chalks, natural resources

What to do
This is the same as the Celtic/Viking village activity (see page 72). But I think it's worth putting it in both sections due to the quality of talk, thinking and problem solving that comes out of the work, and how the activity is approached differently by different aged children.

Lots of historical enquiry, and negotiation, required to build an ancient city

Give the children a fact sheet with six or seven pieces of information that we know about the design of Ancient Baghdad. Explain the difference, in historical terms, between fact and interpretation. Explain that the facts that are on the sheets are known to be true and discuss how we can be certain. Then talk about how people can interpret information in different ways and this can lead to different conclusions being drawn. Explain that the aim of the lesson is for the children to stick to the given facts, but use them to work out what Ancient Baghdad might have looked like. They can use chalks, LEGO®, and any other natural resources to create the city – and they need to be able to justify the choices and decisions they make.

I presented the problem to a class of Year 6s, and before we even got to the playground I had two lads talking to me about the military area in Baghdad. They were discussing the relative merits of it being either at ground level (so the army could react quickly), or the need to be higher (so they could see potential attackers more easily). This seemed to me to be a piece of fantastic historical enquiry and reasoning that was shared with the rest of the class and prompted higher order thinking and discussion in many others.

Later in the lesson, while the children were designing, they were recalling information from the quiz we had done at the beginning of the session and also asking more questions. We had great discussions about rubbish (what sort would have been created, where it would have gone, how it compares to now). We discussed the location of the river (would it go through the centre of the city like the Thames, or round the city?) and what impact that would have on other planning decisions.

I hope the value and depth of this work is obvious. Take photos for evidence, and to support any written work that follows this learning.

Building Bedouin tents

Cross-curricular links
DT, maths, science

Soft skills development
Problem solving, dexterity, team work, resilience

Resources
Sturdy sticks, string, water

What to do
We are lucky that we have trees in our grounds that
have been coppiced and we have sturdy lengths of wood
about 1.5m long that are perfect for this activity. If you
haven't got these on site, you could either contact a
tree surgeon or the town council to see if they can
help. Alternatively, this activity could be carried out with
shorter sticks, as long as they are sturdy enough.

Den building linked to history – children
love it!

Before leaving the classroom, look at some images
of Bedouin tents and discuss who used them and what they were used for. Explain that the
children are going to make their own versions of Bedouin tents outside in the grounds.

Break the work outside into a series of challenges. First, the children have to use string to make
one post/stick stay upright and not wobble. Attaching three bits of string to the top and pulling
them down tightly and fixing them to the ground with pegs (shorter sticks) works, but your
children may come up with other methods. If the ground is hard, provide water to soften it, but
any hammering can be done with sticks.

This normally takes one session. At the start of the next lesson, remind the children of previous
learning and make some links to forces in science. Having pegs at angles leaning away from
the upright, fixing the strings to the pegs as close to the ground as possible and arranging the
strings in triangles from all angles (including the top), makes the structure as strong as possible,
and uses forces to support rather than pull against.

Next, having fixed one post upright, challenge them to do two or three more, so that if a
tarpaulin or sheet were to be spread out, it would spread across the posts.

Give the children a sheet or duvet cover and the challenge is then to use what they have already
learnt to create a shelter big enough for their entire group (three or four) to fit underneath.
There are numerous ways of doing this – it is worth preparing the children for how to deal
with selecting one idea from a number of different ones to prevent the odd falling out when
someone doesn't get their way!

The children love the success most achieve, and often start to decorate their tents if they have
time. They are also usually more than willing to share their expertise to try to make sure others
are also successful.

4 Geography Outdoors

What does the National Curriculum say?

A tutor on my MA course at Winchester University once said that the whole primary geography curriculum could be taught outside. Although this is a situation I may aspire to, I'm certainly not there yet. However, there are many opportunities for working outside with children to teach and learn geography. It is also worth noting that geography is the only part of the National Curriculum that actually stipulates that children should be involved in fieldwork and, as such, going outside is actually a requirement.

The National Curriculum states that 'a high-quality geography education should inspire in pupils a curiosity and fascination about the world and its people that will remain with them for the rest of their lives.' It says that children should develop a knowledge of human and physical geography and, over time, understand the link between the two. One of the aims of the curriculum is to 'collect, analyse and communicate with a range of data gathered through experiences of fieldwork that deepen their understanding of geographical processes'. At key stage 1, the National Curriculum also says that 'first-hand observation' should be used to develop locational awareness. In order to achieve these, I would think that working outside with children, both to gain knowledge and develop skills would be both desirable and essential and, as with science, I see real benefits in children starting to learn geography through exploring the world around them. Beginning with studying their immediate locality means when children come to research alternative locations, and unknown physical and human geography, they have something on which to base their experiences.

In terms of the structure of this chapter, I shall take each aspect of geography and suggest ideas for key stage 1 and then key stage 2, so it is easier to see the flow and development between the two. On occasions however, some of the ideas, if adapted, are suitable for both key stages.

As I have worked through this chapter, it has become increasingly apparent that there are really important links between the different strands in geography. When planning the geography curriculum, identifying these links will not only make the children's experiences more interesting and valuable, but it will save you a lot of time as well. In addition, exploiting the links between geography and other curriculum areas will allow for relevant and context-based writing and maths. Learning in conjunction with other areas can, in my opinion, enrich and deepen the children's experiences and help them to see learning as part of a whole, not as an exclusively subject specific experience.

Locational knowledge: Key stage 1 and 2

Locational awareness in the National Curriculum is very much based on learning names, places and features. There are a number of ways of doing this, all of which can be adapted to different ages of children. Moreover, I have to say, all the children who have ever worked on them have loved all these ideas.

These activities can be adapted so they are appropriate for different ages and abilities learning continents and oceans, countries in the UK and their capital cities, counties and cities, countries in Europe and the Americas, and topographical features. For ease of reading, I shall base the activities on learning the names of European countries.

Country quiz

Cross-curricular links
It depends how this area of learning fits within topics, but science, maths and English all provide possible links.

Soft skills development
Memory, resilience, determination, team-work

Resources
Strips of paper, pencils, maps for recording, information cards, clipboards

What to do
Start by letting the children work out what they know already. Simply ask the children to write down, in about three minutes, names of the European countries. Before going outside, it is useful to know their current knowledge and be able to extend and support accordingly. When I asked Year 4 to do this recently, one boy knew 15 countries, none of the others knew more than three, and some could only manage England. Go through the lists and counter any misconceptions, for example, the difference between countries and cities, and that countries form different continents.

Having established the benchmark number of countries known, set a challenge that by the end of the lesson they need to know at least 10 more.

Ask the children to work in pairs and give them a map of Europe with each country numbered. Firstly, have a look at the map, locate the United Kingdom, and make sure all understand that the lines are boundaries between countries and all the different shapes are different countries. Name a few so the children have an idea of what they are looking for. Hanging around the school grounds, I have a card for each country with the number at the top, then the name of the country, the flag, and the capital city. The flag and capital city are to enable extension for any children who are particularly knowledgeable.

| 13. |
| Slovenia |
| |
| Ljubljana |

Example of a country quiz card

Ask the children to leave their maps and clipboards near you in a central place, run to find a card, remember the number and name, and return to fill it in on their maps. Talk to the children about developing memory skills by reading, speaking, listening and repeating – and it works!

Leaving clipboards where you are also means you can see that all the children are engaged, and question and prompt those that need it. For the last ten minutes, perhaps let the children take clipboards with them to try to find the remaining information.

Back in class, read the names they have found, and give them another three or four minutes to rewrite the list of countries they know – the results are usually impressive. It is worth repeating this list-making, maybe as a register task, on a regular basis for a few weeks, so names become established.

A fun, effective and practical way of learning European countries

I do think it is worth noting here that I have had very reluctant readers and writers taking the lead in their pair when carrying out this work. Children who struggle to read key words can miraculously sound out Estonia. Others, who use all avoidance techniques possible when writing in class, refuse to share the pencil as they want to do all the writing. This is really valuable, as when these children then show reluctance back in the classroom, they can be reminded of their enthusiasm and success outside, which can often spur them on to greater things inside.

Drawing maps

Cross-curricular links
It depends how this area of learning fits within topics, but science, maths and English all provide possible links.

Soft skills development
Attention to detail, communication, resilience

Resources
Atlases, chalks

What to do
This is a really simple but effective outdoor activity which requires precious little organising, but can produce some fantastic learning. I would do it after the previous activity, when the children have already increased their knowledge of European countries.

The language children use when drawing maps can be as impressive as the finished product

Simply ask the children to find the page in the atlas that shows all the European countries, hopefully using the contents or index! Have a look so the children can remind themselves of previous learning, but also start to concentrate more on the location of the countries as well as their names. Once the children have had some valuable time looking at and discussing the map, take them outside and ask them to recreate the map of Europe on the playground, using chalks. It is a fascinating exercise where the children have to talk, negotiate and discuss size, shape and location of countries. They also have to decide where to start, whether different coloured chalks might be useful, and some may decide that using symbols and keys are a good idea. There is also the option to restart if the children need to (remember Austen's Butterfly).

In the end, the children's maps may not look particularly like the original – but does that matter? I would suggest not. I am of the opinion that the discussion, the constant referring to the atlases and using the names of the countries will be the most valuable part, making the process much more important than the finished product.

Place knowledge: Key stage 1

Place knowledge requires comparing 'the human and physical geography of a small area of the United Kingdom and of a small area of a contrasting non-European country'. I shall assume that the area of the United Kingdom will be that in which the school is based, and the following ideas are made because of that assumption.

Investigating maps

Cross-curricular links
It depends how this area of learning fits within topics, but science, maths, English and history all provide possible links.

Soft skills development
Attention to detail, planning, explaining and describing

Resources
Maps of the local area, chalks

What to do
I think it is really important that children develop an increasing knowledge of and – hopefully – pride in where they live. Give the children time to look at and discuss maps of the local area set out on tables. You might not need to intervene or give instructions for a good ten minutes or so, as the children may well just become absorbed and investigate the maps with no whole class guidance. The discussions are really interesting and it is amazing how much the children can work out from the maps, if they are given the time to look and talk.

Drawing route maps is much easier on the playground where there's lots of space

Then challenge the children to draw, on the playground, their route to school. Ask them to draw on all the things they can remember seeing on the route, thinking about the order of what they see, what is next to each other, which side of the road they are on etc. Model this on the whiteboard first, giving the perfect opportunity for the children to see why we do this on the playground and not on paper – there is never enough space when working on paper, whereas the playground provides a limitless canvas.

If some of the children travel in cars, or they travel too far for them to draw their route to school, then ask them to draw the location around the school or their home. This is best done if the children have had the chance to walk the area around school, and have photos that can remind them of where they have been.

Investigating the local area

Cross-curricular links
It depends how this area of learning fits within topics, but science, maths, English and history all provide possible links.

Soft skills development
Questioning, care, social awareness

Resources
Pencils, recording sheets, clipboards

What to do
It is possible to do this activity from within the school grounds, but it would certainly be improved by going further afield and visiting the locality around the school (but this would obviously involve risk assessments and extra adults, although no extra expense).

In order to have an understanding of the human and physical geography of the area where the school is located, you can look at the amenities, movement of traffic and people, and simple land use. You can work together to devise a simple tally chart, considering what you might see – but it might be worth doing this having had a walk around the grounds, looking out beyond the school boundaries first, so the children make their suggestions based on knowledge, rather than guessing. Things on your list will depend on your location, but you could include, for example, different types of buildings (by usage), number of trees, cars (parked and being driven), people walking past, telegraph poles, electricity pylons, post boxes etc. Having compiled the list, you can go outside and ask the children to count and record what they see. This data can then be presented in a number of ways (for example bar charts, pictograms, even line graphs if data is collected over time), potentially developing into some maths work.

It is also possible to collect and present some of your data on maps. We have laminated maps of the school grounds, but they are relatively small, in the middle of an A3 sheet of paper. This allows for the outside blank space on the sheets to be used for extending the map or making notes, which would be ideal for elements of this task. The children could draw what they see onto the maps and count them after. In this way you have not only the number of different items, but also their location.

Going further afield would allow for more data to be collected. If this isn't possible, then using maps and photos of the local area would suffice, but again, working outside allows the maps and photos to be placed and orientated properly. This would give the children more of a feel for where things are in reality and how they all fit together.

The data gathered from this activity would allow for direct comparisons with another area of the world, making a valuable study.

Field sketches

Cross-curricular links
It depends how this area of learning fits within topics, but science, maths, English and history all provide possible links.

Soft skills development
Questioning, care, observation skills

Resources
Chalks

What to do
Model on an interactive whiteboard how to split the landscape page into three parts horizontally so the children can then concentrate on

Field sketches out in the 'field' – where better?!

what is in the foreground, mid ground and in the distance. Discuss what should and shouldn't be included in a field sketch (same principle as for maps) and then start adding details. You can either use a photo as a stimulus or a view out of a window. Go outside and ask the children to make field sketches on the playground with chalk. Alternatively, they can be done on paper, but they do really need to be done outside! It is a great activity that encourages children to look closely at their immediate surroundings, taking notice of the smaller details that might not usually be seen. It is an activity that ties in beautifully with work on investigating the local area.

Place knowledge: Key stage 2

This study is similar to the work in key stage 1, but the children are looking at a region in the United Kingdom and comparing it to regions in a different European country and another in North or South America. This study ought to be carried out by visiting part of the region in the United Kingdom you are investigating, carrying out surveys and collecting data, taking photographs and using maps to consider land use. Fieldwork is vital to the success of this study.

Human and physical geography: Key stage 1

At key stage 1, this element of geography involves developing a greater understanding of areas of the world and understanding what is meant by key geographical vocabulary, most of which many children would have come across before. It also involves looking at weather patterns, which I won't go into detail about as it ties in nicely with work in science explained previously.

Developing use of basic geographical vocabulary

Vocabulary: beach, cliff, coast, forest, hill, mountain, sea, ocean, river, soil, valley, vegetation, season, weather, city, town, village, factory, farm, house, office, port, harbour, shop

Cross-curricular links
Other areas of geography, English, maths

Soft skills development
Logic, planning, attention to detail

Resources
Vocabulary cards, photos, chalks

What to do
Link this to work on maps that we have already talked about. It is important that children know key vocabulary and understand what it relates to as I have seen it can give them a sense of empowerment and confidence. Therefore, use a range of photos and vocabulary cards to allow the children to pair them up and see what each word relates to and looks like. Discussion can then follow and features can be considered. If the photos are laminated, notes can be written on the back using whiteboard pens, and then this activity can easily take place outside. Encourage the children to draw maps of imaginary places, using as many of the features as they feel is reasonable and appropriate. This activity will enable you to see easily if the children really understand the different features depending on their position on a map. For example, port, harbour, sea, cliff, coast, beach and ocean could obviously all be in the same vicinity. It would be interesting too if they can explain why they have omitted other features as this would also show a level of understanding.

I spoke to some children about the difference between working on paper and working on the playground, and which they preferred. They rightly said that there was a place for both, but doing maps on the playground, according to them, was an absolute must. They cited a number of reasons including having a limitless amount of space, being able to work collaboratively with ease, and being physically active. It was great to have the children confirming what I believed to be true!

Human and physical geography: Key stage 2

At key stage 2, the areas of study become more widespread but there remains the option of linking these areas of work to other areas of the geography curriculum, and other curriculum areas, notably science.

Rivers

This activity is also explained in the history section (Ancient Egypt). However, as this study also works beautifully in the geography section, I make no apology for repeating it here.

Cross-curricular links
Other areas of geography, science, maths

Soft skills development
Enquiry, observation, reasoning, collaboration

Resources
Vocabulary cards, LEGO®, water, water pots

What to do
This learning works beautifully as long as you have some sort of slope within your school grounds. It

A favourite activity – all make a label for their own rivers, then one gets 'flooded'!

doesn't have to be steep, it just needs to allow movement of water (we work on a small grass bank that flows from the field onto the playground). The children work in groups and start by deciding where the source of their 'river' is going to be. Label the source with one of the vocabulary cards and start pouring water gently from the source, watching carefully where and how the water flows down the bank. If the children spot other river features (meanders, tributaries, mouth…) they can label them with other vocabulary cards. To develop this further, and starting to consider land use and environmental effects, ask the children to place LEGO® houses near the river. They have to be close enough to get the benefits of the water, but not be at risk of flooding. Placement can be tested by tipping more water down the channel and seeing if any houses do, in fact, get wet.

You could also simulate a flood by tipping a bucket full of water down the river channel in one go. Many areas of our country have experienced floods, and they are regularly in the news. The children's excitement at the amount of water and 'houses' floating away can easily be focused through watching videos of this happening for real. This work can lead to writing opportunities, can be linked to investigating local planning proposals, links nicely to topic work on Ancient Egypt.

There is an additional activity that would reinforce work on rivers. If you have a range of different size stones and sand it is possible to make a model of a river channel, thinking about where stones of different sizes are found, and why. This is a very memorable learning experience which takes thinking beyond the basic 'naming of parts' to a situation where children have to explain what is where, and why. It is an activity that would be good to do following a trip to a river, but if this is not possible, then use photographs instead.

Cleaning dirty water

Cross-curricular links
Other areas of geography, science, maths

Soft skills development
Thinking, resilience, team work, communication, analysis

Resources
Plastic drinks bottles, fabric, dirty water, sieves, filter paper

What to do
You can also work on a geography/science activity when studying rivers. Set up a survival scenario with your class that links both geography and science: they are by a river and have run out of water. They have an empty water bottle and the resources around them – what can they do to clean the water from the river to make it drinkable? Have some dirty water (made dirty with a range of materials from mud to leaves) and challenge the children to clean it. You can just use the materials they have available, or you can add sieves and filter paper at some stage if you wish. I also have fabric available as they could, in a real situation, use their clothes to clean the water.

Do make it clear that however successful the children are, the water will still not be clean enough to drink – it should be obvious why, but the discussion about bacteria is an interesting one to have.

A learning experience to bring out the Bear Grylls in your class!

Volcanoes

Cross-curricular links
Other areas of geography, science, maths, history

Soft skills development
Enquiry, observation, reasoning, collaboration, attention to detail

Resources
Small plastic bottles, vinegar, bicarbonate of soda, red food colouring (not essential), trowels, LEGO®, twigs

What to do
Although making exploding volcanoes in school doesn't replicate the way they work in reality and as long as this is made clear, I still think there is value in making them as what you can observe is how the environment around the 'volcano' changes when an eruption occurs. So, in advance of this learning experience outside, make sure the preparatory work is done inside. Investigate different volcanoes, look at their structure, name the different parts, know why they erupt and watch videos which show evidence of the eruptions and the consequences.

Explain that the volcanoes that will be made outside will erupt due to a chemical reaction rather than a natural disaster. Put some bicarbonate of soda into each of the plastic bottles and then dig some holes to submerge up to half of the bottle. Pack soil around the rest of the bottle so that it looks like a mountain/volcano, making sure no soil goes inside the bottle (it might be worth keeping the lid on until this work has been carried out). At this stage, trees in the form of sticks can be added to the environment, and LEGO® can be used to make settlements. In order to make the volcano erupt, add vinegar (with red food dye added if you wish) to the neck of each bottle and stand back!

Observe and photograph the eruption, and see what impact it has on the vegetation and settlements that have been created around the volcano.

It is worth practicing this in advance to make sure you get the quantities of bicarbonate of soda and vinegar correct so that the results are impressive and allow for the wow factor.

The water cycle

Cross-curricular links
Science, maths, drama

Soft skills development
Enquiry, observation, reasoning, collaboration, questioning

Resources
Chalk, quiz about the water cycle, clipboards, pencils, recording sheets

Reinforcing knowledge by creating a labelled diagram

What to do
Use a quiz in the school grounds to make sure all the children have all the basic facts and knowledge of the key vocabulary they need in order to understand the water cycle. Each card has one piece of information about the water cycle, with key words in bold and illustrations to aid understanding. The children can have recording sheets that either have questions on with the answers to be found on the information cards, or they could be diagrams of the water cycle with information missing that can be filled in. This is a good way to ensure there is a shared understanding of basic information (refer to the bottom two levels on Bloom's Taxonomy – see Bibliography for link) before moving on to a more investigative and creative approach.

The children could draw the journey of a rain drop in chalks on the playground, or present it as a piece of drama.

Then investigate what happens to the water when it rains within the school grounds. Look at the different surfaces and see if the children can predict the flow of water, considering where it goes to immediately and then afterwards when it may be out of sight. The responses will obviously be different depending on where the water lands, but thoughts could be recorded on maps of the school grounds. In addition, observations of puddles can be carried out to aid understanding of the precipitation and evaporation process, but I would encourage you get the children to think about what happens to water that falls on surfaces other than the playground.

You can also test evaporation in different areas of the school grounds, again working scientifically, by putting equal amounts of water in different places and observing how long they take to evaporate. The opportunities for fair testing and recording in this experiment are valuable, and the children will learn that, even within a small location, there are big differences in the environment. Drawing conclusions from this experiment may seem quite straight forward, but it does allow for more complex and detailed thinking.

Land use

Cross-curricular links
English, maths, history

Soft skills development
Enquiry, observation, reasoning, collaboration, questioning

Resources
Clipboards, pencils, recording sheets

What to do
Land use is an interesting concept that can be linked to historical studies as well as thinking about the present and future plans. As often in geography, start with the local area as it has direct relevance to the children, and then broaden investigations to areas beyond their direct knowledge.

A combination of direct observation and use of maps and photographs, combined with what the children already know about where they live provide a good starting point for investigating land use. Ask the children to record different possibilities for land use and come up with an agreed class list. Take the children outside and go to different positions in the school grounds so you can see different views. Record the different uses of land that can be seen from the school. This can be shown using field sketches (see page 89), a tally chart, or recorded on maps of the grounds. Whilst outside, it is also worth taking and investigating maps of the local area and getting the children to link what is on the maps to the reality of what is on the ground. In addition to becoming more adept at using maps, it will also allow them to identify how land is used in places they can't actually see. This will be especially important in areas where buildings, other natural or built obstructions impede the view.

Having spent time outside observing and recording, information can be taken back into the classroom, analysed and compared to different locations that you are studying. This links directly with the 'place knowledge' part of the geography curriculum.

Geographical skills and fieldwork: Key stage 1

I am not going to go into much detail about this section, as most of the skills and fieldwork can be carried out through other areas of the geography curriculum. Working within a context will ensure that they have much more meaning and relevance than working on them as stand-alone elements. Having said that, we haven't yet discussed directions or grid references so we shall now investigate those.

Using a compass

Use simple compass directions (north, south, east and west) and locational and directional language (for example, near and far; left and right), to describe the location of features and routes on a map.

Cross-curricular links
Maths

Soft skills development
Listening, planning, co-operation, following and devising instructions

Resources
Chalks

What to do
An initial game of North, South, East and West is a good starting point for work on direction. Draw a big compass in the middle of the playground, with the arrows pointing in the right direction geographically. This means you can actually tell the children that if they start walking north and keep going they will really get to the North Pole.

To play the game, just ask the children to stand in the middle of the playground and run in the direction you state. You can have the whole class moving at once, or if you need to have only small groups moving at one time, split into groups according to gender, house groups or other methods. You can also include distance in this, by asking them to travel a given number of paces in one direction. Depending on the age, ability and experience of your children, you could begin to introduce north-east, north-west, south-east and south-west by asking the children what instructions you would have to give if you wanted them to travel between the given points. The children, possibly with some guidance, will probably come up with the right terminology and then you can draw these points on the playground too and increase your range of instructions.

To link directional work to map work, you could draw a big fictional map on the playground, with different features marked on and ask the children to move from one to another saying which direction they are moving in. The children can then take ownership of this and set each other challenges, leaving you freer to observe and support. This work can be easily recorded if necessary with the children recording where they are travelling to and from, and the direction they are moving – two symbols and a letter is all that is needed. For example 'PC north'. In addition, if the children have had experience of drawing maps before, they could also draw the map itself, consolidating their work on using symbols and keys and saving you the preparation time.

Geographical skills and fieldwork: Key stage 2

More compass work

Use the eight points of a compass, four and six-figure grid references, symbols and key (including the use of Ordnance Survey (OS) maps) to build their knowledge of the United Kingdom and the wider world.

Cross-curricular links
Maths

Soft skills development
Listening, planning, co-operation, following and devising instructions

Resources
Chalks, recording sheets, clipboards, pencils, OS symbol cards

What to do
The use of OS maps, keys and symbols is discussed in the next section but do combine their use with grid references. Draw grid lines on the playground and number them (it doesn't take as long as you might fear). You can draw some symbols in certain places and ask the children to give the correct co-ordinates (either verbally or recorded). They can then draw in other symbols, or place symbol cards in specific places and ask working partners to say where they are. As long as the grids you have drawn are big enough, this can easily be developed to six-figure as well as four-figure grid references.

The same grid and symbols can then be used to give directions using eight points of the compass – and I think key stage 2 would be the time to introduce real compasses. Some children find them quite difficult to use, but enough in your class would have had experience of them in cubs or scouts, so you'll be able to employ experts to help the others!

Once the children have had practical, first-hand experience of co-ordinates and directional work outside, it will be a lot easier and more meaningful to develop it inside, linking it to the other geographical themes you are working on.

Using standardised symbols

Cross-curricular links
It depends how this area of learning fits within topics, but science, maths, English and history all provide possible links

Soft skills development
Logic, planning, attention to detail

Resources
Maps, OS Maps, charts of selected OS symbols, envelopes containing OS symbols drawn on individual cards, chalks

Children love creating maps using 'proper' OS symbols. The results are amazing!

What to do
Introduce standardised symbols in key stage 2. If time permits, it might be worth spending half an hour drawing maps using whatever symbols the children choose (as suggested in the key stage 1 ideas). Then, if the children look at each other's maps, they are likely to see that it can be difficult to interpret them as they don't know what all the different symbols mean.

If you don't have time for the children to do this themselves, create some maps to show them on the whiteboard and ask them to guess what the different symbols mean. You are likely to get a range of different possibilities for the same symbol, which will lead nicely into introducing why standardised symbols are so important.

If you don't have time, this can be explained quite easily with different maps on the whiteboard.

Then have a look at OS maps and ask the children to use the keys to identify what the different symbols mean and identify as many of them as they can on the maps.

In order for the children to become confident with recognising and remembering the symbols, I play a game on the whiteboard, and another outside. The whiteboard is a quick one: have the symbols drawn, but covered and then do a slow reveal asking the children to identify which symbol is being uncovered. Outside, split the class into groups standing at one side of the playground, and have all the symbols drawn on bits of card in envelopes at the other side. The children take it in turns to run to an envelope, take a card, run back to their group and they decide together which symbol it is. The second person then takes that card back to the envelope and returns to the group with another card. This carries on for as long as necessary, with cards being repeated, until you are happy that most children can recognise most cards. It is great fun, collaborative, supportive – and keeps the children warm outside even on a cold day.

Then start drawing maps using the OS symbols and chalks. The children work in small groups and design a village including all the things they think are important. They have to consider where roads go, the location of key buildings and open spaces, where car parks need to be located etc. The quality of discussion can be fantastic. Challenge the children to explain the choices they are making, which further improves the quality of work.

Another exciting element happens when two groups start to join their work together because their villages have grown to such an extent. Maps develop from villages to towns, then become cities, which can grow into conurbations. The discussions around this can be really enlightening with children thinking about the human consequences, as well as the geographical and environmental implications. All of this work, which is happening in the abstract, can then usually be linked to planning proposals, applications and building work that is going on in your local area. This makes it a concrete issue which will impact on the children and their families. You can imagine the quality of impassioned writing that could come from this outside experience.

5 Art and Design Outdoors

What does the National Curriculum say?

Art and design in the National Curriculum is covered in two pages. The purpose of study indicates that 'a high-quality art and design education should engage, inspire and challenge pupils, equipping them with the knowledge and skills to experiment, invent and create their own works of art, craft and design.' The aims go into more detail, outlining the four strands that need to be addressed during the primary phase:

- producing creative work;
- becoming proficient in artistic skills;
- evaluating and analysing creative works;
- learning about artists and designers.

There are obvious connections between the strands that can be exploited. When using the outside for art, I would suggest that looking at work by chosen artists, and finding out a little about them before producing creative work and becoming proficient in artistic skills is one way forward which links all the strands together. I would also add that working outside in art and design, as with other subjects, links directly to the purpose of inspiring and challenging pupils. We have to remember that although some children are happy working in a classroom, not all are, and certainly not all are happy in that environment all of the time. In my experience, finding opportunities to carry out artwork outside can and does inspire pupils.

The way the art curriculum is written suggests to me that most schools will link their artwork to other curriculum areas, which is what we certainly do at Anstey. As such, I shall try to make the ideas as general as possible so they can be applied to a range of topics and other curriculum areas.

Using the outside for artwork can happen in two main ways:

- using materials found outside to actually produce the art itself;
- using the outside as a stimulus for work that is carried out on paper or using other media.

I shall make suggestions for both here but do use your imaginations and knowledge of your own grounds – these ideas are, as always, only starting points and need to be adapted to suit your setting, children and curriculum. I shall not, on this occasion, give different ideas for key stage 1 and key stage 2. Apart from the use of sketch books at key stage 2, the development through the primary stage is really 'mastery' of skills, which can be learnt through specific teaching points and practical experience. As such, it will be possible to adapt the ideas given here to different topics, ages and experiences of the children.

I have also suggested a few artists who I have used with children, to whom they have responded well – but I am not a specialist art teacher and the ideas I have given are very limited. You may well know many more that would provide a good stimulus for your children.

Using materials found outside

Environmental art (land art)

Cross-curricular links
Can be linked to many topics,
especially history

Soft skills development
Attention to detail, care, resilience

Resources
A range of natural resources,
camera, PowerPoint of Land Art
examples

What to do
If you haven't come across it
already, have a look at the work
carried out by artists such as Andy
Goldsworthy, Tim Pugh and Richard
Long. They all use what they find in
the natural environment to develop the most stunning examples of environmental or land art.
They work in a range of outdoor settings, using different materials, depending on the place and
season. When looking at their work, do discuss it in an artistic manner as well as asking for an
emotional response. Elements of line, colour, shape and texture can be explored.

Creating land art involves a thoughtful process, and produces
stunning outcomes

The children's responses to seeing work by these artists is priceless – real awe and wonder
moments in the classroom before you even go outside!

Once you have explored 'land art', and maybe found out a little about the artists themselves
(although this can come later), the work outside can commence. You can challenge the children
to be creative using items they find in the grounds and create art for the sake of art – the
the results will be stunning. Encouraging children to produce work that is totally their own
response to such beautiful stimuli is very rewarding and successful so that even your more
reluctant artists should be engaged and proud of what they achieve.

The season and weather conditions will certainly have an impact on what is produced, as will
the availability of resources in your grounds. But if you are short of resources, then do collect
your own, or ask the children to. I did some INSET recently at a school that has a big outside
space, but no trees, so I took sticks, pine cones and a variety of leaves with me. It's not quite
the same as the children collecting their own, but it does the job. (It is also worth adding that
all these resources were used not only for art during the INSET day, but also for numerous
maths activities, and some language ones too – collect and store for future use!)

Following on from this (or as a lesson in its own right) if you wish to link it to topic work, there are plenty of opportunities. Ask the children to create Islamic patterns (linking to work on Ancient Baghdad) and mosaics (linking to work on the Romans). Doing this in the autumn term when there is a wide range of coloured leaves available works well, but shape and form at other times of the year can produce work that is just as beautiful. Do be explicit about the link between the land art and the outcomes you are looking for, and make the elements of art explicit too. Do you want the children to concentrate on colour, shape, line, or a combination of these? Just because the children aren't working on paper, it doesn't 'dumb down' the art the children should be producing, especially if you have looked at stunning examples first, and analysed the artistic elements these artists have used.

3D work

Cross-curricular links
Can be linked to many topics, especially history, geography and science

Soft skills development
Creativity, imagination, care, attention to detail, problem solving

Resources
Clay, clay tools, newspaper or clay boards, sticks, other natural resources

What to do
Regardless of the focus, I try to do clay work outside. It means all the mess is outside and the children have much more space to move around than they would if they were in the classroom. Pots or tiles linked to history can be made. I have had children working in groups to make walls for houses which are then put together, all linked to a local history unit where observational drawings of buildings (also outside) have been done to inform clay work.

The framework for a 3D Christmas tree – learning that can be developed to fit many situations

The environment in which you are working can inspire clay and other 3D work. Perhaps, having identified trees in your grounds, do some observational drawings and make clay trees, working on shape, texture and proportion. It is possible to make trees or figures with clay from the local environment. There are woodlands near me where I can collect red clay, and a river where I can collect grey clay (but I only ever take small amounts, and very infrequently), but you may not be so lucky. If not, use clay which is purchased through County Supplies or similar. When they are finished, the models can be photographed individually, placed in a small coppice or at the base of a tree and photographed again. At that point they can be left them outside. They may last a few weeks and the children can watch their demise! Alternatively, you can easily keep them and have something for the children to take home.

You can also work on structures with children outside. Leading up to Christmas, I challenged the children to make Christmas trees using any materials they could find. You will probably get quite traditional 2D pyramids and 3D triangular-based pyramids, as well as some very abstract and interesting creations. The children love the challenge, and the opportunity to work in groups on large-scale work which allows them to use their creativity within a framework. Although this work was linked to Christmas, it can easily be adapted to link to other work.

Using the outside as stimulus

Observational drawing and painting

Cross-curricular links
Can be linked to many topics, especially history, geography and science

Soft skills development
Attention to detail, care, precision, observational skills

Resources
Pencils (or pens, charcoal or paints), paper or sketch books, clipboards, magnifying glasses

What to do
Observational drawing is an important part of art, and teaches so many skills that are transferable and important if children are to be successful learners.

Observation skills, drawing and/or painting techniques need to be taught and practised, but once the children have appropriate knowledge and confidence, the outside world offers so many opportunities for drawing and painting.

Leaves, pine cones and bark are all amazing for concentrating on line quality. Flowers are great for colour work. Insects and mini-beasts can provide stimulus for both creative and scientific drawings. Different rocks and stones allow for work on colour and texture. Even the insides of sticks which can be seen after whittling can produce beautiful patterns that could provide the impetus for some stunning observation drawing.

The items that are being drawn can often be taken inside if required, but there is something quite special about working in situ, at least initially. Ask the children to look around and find what they want to draw and what they are interested in (you can give them parameters if necessary). Give them a magnifying glass so they can look at it properly before they start drawing or painting as a reminder that observational drawing is much more observation than drawing! Then set them to work.

Feedback can be really important in order to support children in moving forward, so don't forget Austin's Butterfly – I often show the video to remind children not only how much progress can be made, but also how to give constructive feedback and also how to receive it (see Bibliography for link)!

There are a variety of artists who can inform your work, depending on what your focus is. Georgia O'Keefe's studies of flowers are just stunning and certainly worth a look, and there is 'Sunfowers' by Van Gogh which is also very accessible. Henri Rousseau's work includes both flora and fauna and is liked by children, but fits in especially well with topics related to the rainforest and jungles (alternative locations). Copies of *The Natural History of Selbourne* by Gilbert White provide some beautiful close up images of birds and other animals that could be used to inspire your children. Different editions were illustrated by different people so it is worth looking through different options.

Landscapes and cityscapes

Cross-curricular links
Can be linked to many topics, especially history, geography and science

Soft skills development
Attention to detail, care, precision, observational skills

Resources
Pencils (or pens, charcoal or paints), paper or sketch books, clipboards, camera

What to do
The focus of this style of work will be totally dependent on your setting, or where you are when you are carrying out this work. Wherever you are, in the grounds or on a school trip, do make sure you have done preparation work first, so your children have the skills to be able to do the drawing.

There are any number of artists who are worth investigating to prepare the children, including Eric Ravilious, John Constable, Monet, Cezanne and Matisse – the artist you chose is really down to your own preference, who you think the children will be most inspired by, and what you want them to achieve. In terms of cityscapes, have a look at some contemporary work by Stephen Wiltshire or the more traditional Lowry, both of whom will provide some interesting stimulus.

Make sure that the children are completely clear about what they should achieve while they are out. Are they creating small sketches in their sketchbooks to work with at a later date, or are you asking them to produce a complete 'first draft' sketch that can be developed later, perhaps with the use of photos? But the important thing is that, if you want children to attempt landscapes or cityscapes then they need to be able to, at some point, work outside and do so first hand.

Big art inspired by artists

Playground art

Cross-curricular links
Can be linked to many topics, especially history, geography and English

Soft skills development
Attention to detail, care, ability to work on a different scale, co-operation

Resources
Chalks, charcoal, camera

What to do
At Anstey, we do a topic called Totally Urban – a geography topic that compares different locations, concentrating on London and New York. As part of outside learning we look specifically at the work of Roy Lichtenstein, but also consider the work of Andy Warhol and graffiti. However, the principles of playground art can be adapted to different artists and different topics – as long as you are happy using chalks and charcoal as the medium to produce your work. I shall use Roy Lichtenstein as an example.

Investigate the features of Lichtenstein's work and consider what makes it so unique. The children are then challenged to create, on the playground, a piece of work inspired by the man himself. Some chose to try to replicate a Lichtenstein original, others attempt their own work which uses the same features. All work is on a much larger scale than a piece of paper would allow, and children can collaborate and talk in a manner that would be almost impossible in the classroom. The results are generally fabulous.

The work on graffiti outside is preceded by debate in the classroom as to whether graffiti is art or vandalism. Discussion becomes very impassioned written argument, encouraging and enabling the children to take sides and argue their point of view. The children are then taught various graffiti art techniques that are practiced and developed in their sketchbooks.

Take the next step to make their graffiti real, by taking their work outside. It can either be done in chalks, for a temporary art installation, or if their work is worthy, it can be painted as a permanent fixture if you have an appropriate space (for example, a climbing wall that can be painted on, and then repainted white when it is needed for the next class to work on).

Working outside to produce artwork (whether temporary or permanent) does mean there is a large audience. At playtime, all the other children will see what has been produced, and if this is made clear to the children prior to starting, it can really 'up the ante' in terms of quality. And it is so rewarding when children from other classes come and say how much they like the pictures that have been produced.

Pop Art works particularly well on the playground but other styles also look good

6 English Outdoors

What does the National Curriculum say?

Developing children who are confident and competent readers and writers is a hugely important part of what we do in primary schools, and the National Curriculum is very prescriptive about what needs to be learnt and how it is assessed. How these skills and aptitudes are taught is, as always, down to the teacher's and school's discretion.

The National Curriculum states in the purpose of study for English that:

A high-quality education in English will teach pupils to speak and write fluently so that they can communicate their ideas and emotions to others, and through their reading and listening, others can communicate with them.

This is reinforced by the stated aims:

The overarching aim for English in the national curriculum is to promote high standards of language and literacy by equipping pupils with a strong command of the spoken and written word, and to develop their love of literature through widespread reading for enjoyment.

The content of the National Curriculum for English is both demanding and full of content, and it is sometimes, understandably, easy to lose sight of these overall aims and purpose when we are dealing with embedded clauses and fronted adverbials.

My own thoughts, based on both research and personal experience, is that learning outside has a big part to play in not just the development of English, but also the love of and importance of the subject.

If we want to children to read about different environments and contexts, understand them and also write about different scenarios, they need to be able to understand and empathise with them. The 'real-life' experiences of many children today can be somewhat compromised compared to when I was growing up. There are many reasons for this: lack of places to play; increase in the number of cars; stranger danger; and an increase in 'screen time' to name the most obvious. We cannot take for granted that children have had certain experiences – some I have worked with had never walked in the woods, had never seen the sea or built a sandcastle, had never seen or smelt a bonfire. In school, we cannot make up for all the experiences the children may be missing, but we certainly have to take this potential deficit into account and, in the words of my Headteacher, 'do our best to equalise opportunities and experiences'.

I have already mentioned that playing outside encourages and enables a lot more talk than indoor play, and I have seen this with more structured learning too. If by working outside we can help, encourage and support children in using more language, then it isn't too difficult a step to then use that in writing too. It is worth noting that in the purpose and aims of the English National Curriculum, a lot of importance is placed on the development of the spoken word, so by implication we have to make sure opportunities exit for children to develop these skills.

I have had conversations with teachers who say that the best writing they get from their children can often be after a school trip: one recounted how a reluctant writer who usually struggled to write three or four lines produced a side and a half of A4 after a trip to a field studies centre! If we know this can be the case, then we can make the assumption that taking children outside and engaging them in interesting and absorbing work in the school grounds prior to writing can have a similar impact – you are getting the children to write about what they have experienced, rather than something in the abstract.

I know an infant school who, prior to writing about the gunpowder plot, carried out some drama outside. Eight years later, I still have conversations with one of the children who remembers one of the staff, in disguise, creeping up on her and catching her. When she came to writing, the child had such vivid experiences and feelings to base her writing on and her written work was, as a result, stunning. I have worked with children who have held worms for the first time, and then included that sensation in their writing through similes and other descriptive vocabulary that they hadn't previously used. I could quote further examples of how outdoor experiences have informed and inspired writing. However, there are plenty of links already made in previous chapters of this book for inspiration. I know that certain elements of English are probably best taught as discrete elements, but reading and writing can often be linked to other curriculum areas. This not only provides a context for reading and writing, but also has the potential of saving time as two or more curriculum areas are being addressed at the same time. Do go back to other curriculum areas in this book and see where you can draw links between English and the science, history or geography curricula.

So, I think the benefits for language development of taking children outside are compelling and numerous – we need to exploit them as much as we can. However, as reading and writing in primary schools is approached in such individual ways, I will present ideas in this section as broad themes rather than specific lesson ideas. As such, they can then be adapted much more easily to meet the needs of your curriculum and your children.

Reading

Reading outside can be a very easy introduction, for you and the children, to outdoor learning. Taking a box of books, play scripts, or the class reader outside on a sunny day is a perfect way to encourage children to engage in books. Be organised to save time – if you normally have a reading session after lunch, collect books in a box before lunch and meet the children outside at the end of lunch. Do the register outside and then start reading and you have saved five or 10 minutes coming in and going back out again.

Inference and deduction

Research and experience both suggest that inference and deduction skills can be developed in non-or emerging readers as well as those who are fluent and confident. So, using the grounds for inference and deduction with all ages of children is a great idea. I have developed a principle I have seen where pictures are used in the classroom, and children have to use them to investigate the following:

What can I see?	What do I want to know? What do I want to ask?	What can I infer?

Proforma for Developing Inference Skills Outside

This can be done beautifully outside, either giving children a free range of what to look at, or directing them to something specific (picture viewers can be useful for this). Asking the children to describe in as much detail as possible what they can see naturally leads to asking questions. In addition, hypothesising about the answers, based on evidence, will lead to inferences that can be justified and explained.

This learning can be carried out with a pure reading focus, but can also be linked to other subjects too.

Understanding and engagement

Taking children outside to actually feel what it is like to be one of the characters in their book can really make a difference to their understanding and engagement with the text. If a character is walking in the woods, or rolling in the grass then take the children out and let them experience it (don't assume they would have done so already). If a story is set at night, play some blindfold games as I would suspect many children these days haven't experienced real darkness before. The message here is really to consider the book you are reading and asking the children to respond to, and then provide the children with some real experiences so they can relate to it directly. Don't assume that they have done or have felt different things – enhance their learning by giving them experiences which they can then internalise and reflect upon. This will then enable them to really understand the story you are reading, and they will be able to understand and interrogate the text more effectively, thus engaging in higher order reading skills.

Story walks and story lines

Try using story walks and story lines, especially with reluctant readers. The aim is for there to be some physical activity whilst the children are reading. Take a book (or part of one) to pieces, laminate and hang up in the school grounds. Ask the children to read it, a section at a time. How you develop this activity is up to you.

- You could have questions per page read that can be answered either orally or in writing.
- The children could be challenged to find the pages in the right order by solving clues.
- The children could just read for pleasure.
- Words and meanings could be considered, including finding alternatives.

The list of possibilities is endless but it is certainly worth exploring options with children who don't engage in reading normally, as a different environment and the ability to move may just make a difference.

Story lines can be used for sequencing, but again, in a variety of ways. Again, present parts of the story on different pages, and then choose how to use them:

- You can read the story in order and hang pages up as you go, so they can easily be referred back to.
- You can give children all the pages muddled up and ask them to order and hang them up.
- You could use non-fiction writing and decide if order is important (the difference between instructions and non-chronological reports).

Sometimes, as with the story walk, a different approach is enough to engage children for whom reading isn't something they enjoy, or they find difficult, so I would certainly try out different options.

Writing

Creative writing

Creative writing is something that, when appropriate, can be really enhanced by practical experiences. If your school grounds can provide the stimulus for describing a setting or developing a character, then certainly use the possibilities. Drama before writing can help the children really feel their way into a story. Going outside to collect words, phrases, feelings about sounds, sights and smells can really add to the colour that children are able to include in their writing. You may only need a focussed 15 minutes outside to collect and share words and phrases, but the difference in the quality of writing could be huge.

You can also create fantasy areas in your grounds. Something as simple as a little door placed or painted at the bottom of a tree trunk with some stepping stones leading up to it could really spark the imagination of a class. Other ideas would be to leave clues around the grounds which the children had to interpret, specific items hanging from a tree, some graffiti on a wall, a key or an item of clothing on the ground, half hidden under a bush… the possibilities are endless. These ideas do have the added benefit of engaging the children in inference and deduction – in order to write, they need to consider what they have seen, infer and draw conclusions based on the evidence, and then write. You are encouraging higher order thinking skills in a different and hopefully, non-threatening manner.

Story stones

I have also recently become a fan of story stones (similar to story cubes you can buy in bookshops). I have made my own (pebbles from a DIY store and acrylic paints) – a whole set of random designs, and also some themed sets.

How you use them is very much down to personal choice but I have:

- simply let the children use them for a starting point for discussion;
- asked the children to make a simple story using five or six stones;
- worked with children to develop a story plan/mountain (on the playground in chalk, and then on paper if necessary) which shows how the 'stones' move through the story, and encouraged them to make their own. The children then write the story, or part of it, from the plan;
- 'hidden' the stones in the grounds and the children have found them as we have gone for a walk. Their imaginations not only mean they wonder and hypothesise why they are there, but they also start to tell a story as we walk;
- used themed stones to help children retell tales such as *Theseus and the Minotaur*, helping with recall and sequencing for those who need it.

Story stones are very versatile, very tactile and the children love them because of their open-ended nature. I do think they are worth the time spent painting them!

Poetry outside

Poetry outside can be fabulous. Poems are often meant to be read aloud and performed, and children can understand poems better if they can read them aloud. Taking children outside to do this is often preferable to trying in the classroom. The space outside means that children can make more noise without disturbing others, you can model reading and the children can copy, they can work in groups and present their poems, rather than just read them. If it is a long poem, give each group a verse to read, understand and perform, and then put it all together. Discuss as you are going along – by the time the children have to record any responses, they will do so with, hopefully, more confidence and understanding.

Non-fiction writing

Non-fiction writing following trips is usually a real delight for the children to write and for the teacher to read. It makes all the organising and risk assessments worthwhile. Ofsted talk about the best trips being those where the children are prepared in advance for what they are going to do, and use the learning from the trip in their follow up work after. Help the children to be prepared for what is coming as well as following up experiences back in class.

I would suggest that there are a wide range of options for writing following a trip from reports and letters, to producing leaflets, poetry and story writing. You can also use a range of different prompts (as well as the children's memories) – photographs, video clips, maps, mementoes (bought or collected). Children will also remember trips for a long time after the event, so do think about using the trip to inform a range of different learning experiences as the term develops. This means considering having trips in the first half of a term so future work can be informed by the experience (rather than in the last week of term when the trip is really a treat).

The previous chapters of this book provide a huge amount of possibilities for non-fiction writing related to other areas of the curriculum, so do explore these when you are planning your topic and English work. Do consider, when planning your science, history and geography that links can be made and writing opportunities can tie in very easily with other work.

Some good examples are:

- instructions for how to make paints and do cave paintings (Stone Age, page 60);
- argument about the impact of new housing developments (habitats and map work in geography, page 98–99);
- explanation of how flooding affects settlements (rivers, page 74);
- report about the development of ancient settlements (history, page 81–82);
- annotated diagrams of the water cycle (geography, science, page 94).

Do look back through other chapters of this book as the possibilities for writing linked to other curriculum areas are numerous.

Spelling

There is a big emphasis on accurate spelling in the National Curriculum. I can't wave a magic wand and tell you how all children will learn how to spell outside, but working in chalk on the playground can help.

- Writing the words in a big space over and over again is not just satisfying, but does help the children visualise their spellings later. Using different coloured chalk can also help the visualisation process.
- Play hopscotch with letters of the word replacing numbers and the children saying the letters as they hop can work for some.
- Draw out 'stepping stones' with letters in and having to get from one side to the other stepping in letters in the right order is great fun.
- Place letters around an outside space that have to be found to make a word.

I saw a brilliant idea recently where numerous copies of root words written on cards were spread around the playground. There were buckets with prefixes and suffixes stuck to the front of them. The children had to select the root words and then decide which prefix or suffix was appropriate and put it in the right bucket. When all the cards had been allocated, choices were discussed, any corrections made, lists constructed (or photos taken), and then the words were used in sentences to ensure the children understood them in context.

The number of different ways of learning spellings outside is limited only by your imagination, and that of your children. Challenge them to come up with ways that work for them and you will soon have a huge bank of ideas that will inspire you for lots of classes to come.

Grammar

Learning elements of grammar can be approached in the same way as spelling. You are going to want evidence in books but you can still take children outside and chalk on the playground. An activity as simple as using a different coloured chalk to identify the teaching point works well – whether it is working with full stops and capital letters or embedded clauses and expanded noun phrases. Write the main sentence in one coloured chalk and add the teaching focus in another.

Vocabulary and paragraphs

You can develop vocabulary and paragraphs outside. Having read a text, take paragraphs separately and print them on a piece of A4 paper, with individual key words highlighted. Give each child a copy. Hang a range of alternatives to those highlighted words around the grounds for the children to read, discuss and choose from to improve the original paragraph. This is especially great for children who have a limited vocabulary, or for those for whom English is a second language, but it does work well for all.

Also hang sentences around the playground and ask the children to improve them by adding adjectives, adverbs and clauses, and changing the order of sentences. The children build on each other's sentences and can then analyse and evaluate which techniques have been used and how effective they have been. This can have a positive effect on both grammar work and the quality of continuous writing.

7 Maths Outdoors

What does the National Curriculum say?

The programme of study for the primary mathematics curriculum states that:

Mathematics is a creative and highly inter-connected discipline that has been developed over centuries, providing the solution to some of history's most intriguing problems. It is essential to everyday life, critical to science, technology and engineering, and necessary for financial literacy and most forms of employment. A high-quality mathematics education therefore provides a foundation for understanding the world, the ability to reason mathematically, an appreciation of the beauty and power of mathematics, and a sense of enjoyment and curiosity about the subject.

Further to this, the aims state that students:

- 'become fluent in the fundamentals of mathematics, including through varied and frequent practice';
- 'reason mathematically by following a line of enquiry';
- 'can solve problems by applying their mathematics to a variety of routine and non-routine problems with increasing sophistication, including breaking down problems into a series of simpler steps and persevering in seeking solutions'.

If, when planning maths, we are able to keep these principles in mind, it should become clear that maths needs to happen in a range of situations and environments, not just in the classroom. For children to be able to see maths as a 'creative and highly inter-connected discipline' and as 'a foundation for understanding the world', we need to make sure we are teaching it in ways and contexts that enable this to happen.

As with the English chapter, I shall look at ideas within themes across the maths curriculum, rather than giving specific lesson plans. The ideas will be able to be integrated into a sequence of lessons, they will be adaptable both in terms of content and complexity and therefore, when adapted, suitable across the primary age range. As always, the ideas in this chapter are to be seen as a starting point, a stimulus to spark further thoughts so you can make the ideas suitable and appropriate for the children with whom you are working.

I will also add here, as I did in the English chapter, that if you look back through other chapters in this book, you will find a wealth of opportunities for maths linked to other areas of the curriculum. These ideas will certainly mean that your children are 'doing maths' that is inter-connected, and linked to the real world – do go back and look, and try to ensure your planning allows for these connections to be made.

Number

Counting

The youngest of children can sort and count items found outside. One-to-one correspondence is one of the earliest counting skills and this can be done in the real world with anything from leaves and trees to bricks and stepping-stones.

To develop counting in twos, threes or more, sort items into groups of that number and count again. Writing the relevant numbers in chalks will also give practice with fine motor skills and give a visual reminder of what the numbers are in that times table.

Times tables

There is an expectation in the National Curriculum that all children will know their times tables up to 12 × 12, and from 2019, testing times tables will be included in the key stage 2 SATs. This is a big expectation, but we all know that if children do know their times tables then other areas of maths calculations become an awful lot quicker and there are less likely to be mistakes made. So, some possible activities for learning times tables outside

Play games, like hopscotch, can help children learn their tables

Hopscotch

Ask the children to draw out a traditional hopscotch (you may have to model this first) and either put the answers or the questions of the times tables in the squares. The children play the game just saying the numbers, or working out the answers. Children can also work on their own variations of the game, which may include putting the questions/answers in a mixed-up order and using division facts.

Cards

Have the numbers of the times table you are working on printed on A4 card and hang them along a fence. Have all the children counting/chanting the numbers. Then start to turn some round, one or two at a time, so the numbers can't be seen. Give the children clues as to what's on the 'missing cards' (What times table are we working on? What is the middle number? What is the biggest number?) and then chant the numbers again, including the ones that are turned around. Keep going until you have all the cards facing the wrong way and the children are chanting the numbers from memory. You could do a run through with boys

Giving children clues to times tables making learning into a game

Active approaches to learning tables are effective as well as engaging

versus girls, or other combinations to add a competitive edge to the learning, but it keep fast-paced and levels of enthusiasm and engagement will remain high.

Run and find

Make folded cards with the times table question on the outside and the answer on the inside. I have multiple copies of each question so I have at least 40-50 cards in total. On the floor, draw circles with the answers written inside. The children, usually in pairs, get a card, work out the answer, find the circle on the floor and run to it to see if they were correct. They then return the card and get another.

They will end up getting the same question on a number of occasions, but that just reinforces the number fact and makes them quicker. Some will look at the answer instead of working it out, but in my book, that is ok too – the third or fourth time they get that question, they might know the answer without having to look.

You can do the same activity but using division facts, or a mixture of multiplication and division.

I introduced these ideas on a training day for teachers and teaching assistants, and they loved them. What was even better though was when I then challenged them to make up their own games, bearing in mind the children they work with. Their ideas were fabulous. So, as always, use my ideas as starting points and then let your imaginations go wild!

Calculations

Calculations, at all levels, can be done in chalks on the playground to great effect. I have had a number of teachers telling me that when working on a concept inside on paper, a number of children struggled. So, they took them outside and worked on exactly the same style of questions outside, and the majority of the children 'got it'. Why? They put it done to the space, the size of the work and the conversations.

Let me explain more. When working inside in books, it is really only possible for two people to be working together. We often (but not always) have ability groups for maths so those who are struggling are often with others of a similar level of understanding. The work is also restricted by squares in a book and the size of the page. Once outside, the numbers and calculations are drawn much bigger, and all children have the ability to see what others are doing. This means they can pick up on and correct others misconceptions, which also helps them to reinforce and be confident with the process themselves.

For example, I know of a class doing two-by-two digit multiplication. After the teaching points inside and some practice in books, the teacher knew that over half the class were increasing in confidence with the process. She took the class outside and positioned the children around the playground, asking the confident ones to talk and work through the process with those who were still developing an understanding. Roles then reversed and the less confident had a go at working through questions and explaining, with support when needed. The teacher said that there were many differences between working inside and out: there was space for the children to work collaboratively; the calculations were big so groups could all see clearly what was happening; and nearly all the children were talking at once, but there were no noise issues. And by the end of the session, she was confident that all the children had made good progress.

The other thing about being outside is that the children might be able to come up with their own calculation questions based on the environment around them. For example, I can count 53 trees in the school grounds, and I know there are 12 schools in the local area. If they all had the same number of trees, how many would that be? The possibilities are almost endless, and this certainly allows children to take ownership of their learning as well as developing questions related to the topic but in different contexts, allowing for a broadening and deepening of understanding.

Fractions

Using natural resources to find fractions of numbers is a great way of deepening and widening children's experiences. Finding half of 12 by splitting cubes into two sets is fine, but taking the children outside to collect sticks, leaves, stones, or whatever you have available and dividing them into groups gives the children ownership, is more tactic and as such potentially more memorable. This allows them to be physically active while working and ticks the learning objective boxes in the same way.

Measurement

Length, area and perimeter
Being outside gives ample opportunities for measuring in a real-life context.

For younger children, introduce and experiment with longer and shorter using sticks, leaves, or whatever you have. Collect a range of objects and place them in order from shortest to longest to develop this further. You can then find and sort items that are more or less than a metre long (or whatever length suits). Similar activities can be carried out when looking at weight. And there are obvious advantages doing capacity outside!

The content for more formal measuring will depend upon your own setting but take out the rulers, metre sticks, trundle wheels and tape measures. Allow the children to select the right piece of equipment for what is being measured. Make sure the children know how to use the equipment, possibly have some

WAGOLLs (what a good one looks like) of how to record measurements at whatever level you are working at, and then get measuring. In order to assess accuracy, it is worth making sure all the children measure specific items (e.g. the length of a brick, and the height of a planter) that you have already measured.

Work on length can easily be adapted to include perimeter, area and even volume. If the work can be 'real', so the children are working out things for a real problem or purpose, even better. I do think it is important for children to be working out these calculations based on actual objects from time to time, rather than always working on representations in books and being outside gives these opportunities.

It would be very easy to develop all the work on measurement outside so that children had problem solving and reasoning type questions within a real context. You could work out the volume of a planter so you know how much compost to order, or how big football pitches or basketball courts could be if you wanted to fit three onto the field or playground. Your setting will provide numerous real-life opportunities – perhaps go for a walk with a colleague to brainstorm.

Money

Money also comes under measures. In an era where many adults use debit and credit cards for the majority of their financial transactions, making sure children handle money is important. Always try to use real money when working with children, rather than plastic alternatives. I have never had a problem with losing any as the children are always very protective over it and count it on a regular basis. Shop areas can be set up inside classrooms, but they can also be done outside. Outside, you can either have a 'formal shop', or you can put a price on different things in the grounds. Then, all levels of work with money can be carried out including working out the coins to pay with, how much two or more items cost, how much change you will get – the possibilities are endless.

Geometry

2D and 3D shapes

The world is full of shapes so it certainly makes sense to get outside and see them in the real world.

Why not give children a chart with shapes down the side and do tallies for all the different shapes that they can see (this works for 2D and 3D). You could take photos outside with the children and annotate them with the names of different shapes once they are printed off. That way you have the discussion initially and then reinforcement.

Using sticks and masking tape to make different 2D and 3D shapes is so much more reliable than using straws (which bend too easily). Children might have to use secateurs to cut sticks to the correct length, but this provokes good discussion about the number and length of the different edges. It obviously helps to have sticks that are as straight as possible to do this – I go for a walk in the woods every so often and make a collection.

Angles

Physically working on angles outside makes so much sense to children. Standing on the playground and turning to face different directions allows for quarter and half turns, clockwise and anti-clockwise. These turns can then be drawn by the children on the playground to demonstrate how far they have to go.

As formal measurements are introduced, turns can become more accurate, and degrees marked. It is also possible to consider acute, obtuse and reflex angles by drawing on 90°, 180° and 360° degrees and turning within the correct sector for the type of angle required. Doing this work physically and practically alongside the theoretical work in books is more memorable and helps children develop a better and deeper understanding.

You can also take angle finders outside. Glue a 15 cm strip of card at right angles in the middle of a 30 cm strip. Then attach another strip (perhaps in a different colour) to the join, but use a split pin so this strip can rotate. Go outside and use the angle finder to measure angles in the environment – any that fall in the first segment (up to 90°) are acute, the second (between 90° and 180°) are obtuse and those that go beyond the 180° are reflex. Children could then combine the angle finder with a protractor to measure the angles accurately.

Statistics (Year 3 and Year 6)

Although much of the work you do on statistics will be carried out on paper in books, the data you use is much more meaningful and real to the children if they have collected it themselves. The previous chapters in this book provide a wealth of ideas for collecting data and I would certainly be looking to benefit from these. Even if your timetabling means that the children collect data in a science lesson and then don't use it in maths for a few weeks, it will still be a lot more relevant than presenting them with some made up numbers that don't relate to them or any experiences they have actually had.

Bar graphs

With younger children who are being introduced to graphs for the first time, making human bar graphs outside is a great thing to do. Draw the axis, number and label them, and then take it in turns to ask the children to stand in the right place. You can construct them using food or sport preferences, shoe size, height (linking it to work on measures) – anything that is interesting and, if possible, links with other work. Take a photo of the human graph, preferably from an elevated position so when you construct one on paper the children can see that the same information is portrayed.

Venn and Carroll diagrams

Venn and Carroll diagrams, as with calculations, are good things to do in chalk on the playground. There is usually a wealth of natural objects with enough similarities and differences that can be sorted, but if you think there might not be enough, bring in a range of leaves, or pine cones. The size the children draw the diagrams means there will be plenty of opportunity for discussion about not only which section to put the objects in, but also how to label the categories in the first place.

You can develop this work to include sorting numbers (different sections for prime numbers, square numbers, multiples of 3…) and you could even challenge the children with sorting spellings into different sections (a Carroll diagram sorting words with certain numbers of syllables and ending in –cious).

Ratio and proportion (Year 6)

Some children just get ratio and proportion, but others really struggle. Part of that may be that once we get to Year 6, when this is introduced, I think we often work in a much more theoretical manner as we are developing and deepening the skills and knowledge children already have. However, when we introduce a completely new concept, which ratio and proportion will be, for some children there will be a need to go back to the practical. In reality, even if children would understand the concept from a purely book-based theoretical perspective, all children will benefit from the experience of practical work – and it helps them to understand maths in real-life contexts.

Practical work could be linked to a class picnic, sharing out food and drink to given ratios. So, making squash is a perfect example (always try to do liquids outside to reduce the impact of spillages!): 1 part squash to 8 parts water, so 10 ml of squash to 80 ml of water and so on. Make a jug full or individual cups, whichever will allow the children to see the ratio and proportion better. Develop this with food, sharing out crisps, for example, in given proportions, or biscuits and grapes. The options with food are endless, but the children will enjoy the process, get the principle of ratio, and enjoy the eating afterwards. You could even make the eating part of the process – as they eat one thing, what are the ratios now? How many crisps to grapes have they got? Use a range of different combinations (many of which link to other areas of maths too) and keep a record on the floor in chalk to show how much has been used (1:4, so another serving is 2:8, and so on).

Ratio doesn't have to be done with food (although it is fun if it is!). Have a look in your grounds and see what you have that you can compare. Or link it to PE equipment – if every group needs a hoop, three tennis balls and four cones to play a game, how many of each equipment would four groups need? Do work practically first and allow the children to actually set out the equipment, predict, prove and write the ratios. This could then be done as part of a PE lesson without the children even realising they were doing maths, or as a maths lesson in its own right.

Algebra (Year 6)

Algebra is again one of those areas of maths that is a new concept when introduced in Year 6, but unlike ratio, it isn't always as easy to relate it to real life situations. At this level it is purely shapes or letters replacing numbers and how to manipulate the information you have to find out what they represent. Children who are confident with number and number systems are likely to love algebra, others may not and sometimes, working outside initially (which provides temporary results) is less daunting than making permanent recordings in a book.

One thing I have done outside, which has worked, is used natural resources to represent the numbers. For some children, having something practical to work with has taken away some of the 'arghhh' moments and given them a little more confidence.

Starting points will depend on the ability and confidence of the children but it could be as simple as a leaf + a stick = 10, what different values could the leaf and the stick have? Then stick + stick + stick = 36, so how much is the stick worth now? The possibilities are endless, and can certainly be developed to address the complexity of the questions suggested in the National Curriculum. Have a range that you would ask the children to solve and the resources to support this work, and then let the children make up some of their own questions to challenge each other.

Final thoughts

I hope you have found the ideas in this book inspiring. I hope that you are able to see the worth of the concept of outdoor learning, that you are enthusiastic about the learning ideas suggested, and that you are in a position to give some of these ideas a go with your class.

I hope I have given enough ideas and suggestions that you have found a way to begin educating outside, you know where you will start, or that the ideas help you develop your practice. And I hope that even if you're not an outdoor-type, you can see how these learning experiences can benefit your children and, in turn, benefit you too. Believe me, I love nothing better than curling up in front of the television with the fire lit in the evening, but this is always best when I've had a day learning outside with children.

I am sure that your children will love the learning experiences. And, as the experiences of childhood last a lifetime, the more positive, engaging, memorable opportunities we can give children, the more we are adding to their future as well as their current education.

So, good luck, enjoy and get educating outside!

Bibliography and useful links

Seed dispersal video: http://www.bbc.co.uk/education/clips/znvfb9q (see page 24)
Fossils video: https://www.youtube.com/watch?v=TVwPLWOo9TE (see page 39)
Austin's Butterfly: https://www.youtube.com/watch?v=hqh1MRWZjms
Bloom's Taxonomy: https://cft.vanderbilt.edu/guides-sub-pages/blooms-taxonomy/
Wattle and Daub: https://www.youtube.com/watch?v=VIJIFBAAjvE (see page 70)
DfE, (2013) 'The national curriculum in England Key stages 1 and 2 framework document': www.gov.uk/government/publications/national-curriculum-in-england-primary-curriculum
How to draw a maze: https://snapguide.com/guides/draw-a-maze/
White, G. (1977) *The Natural History of Selborne* (Penguin Classics) (although there are many other versions which are illustrated by different people, so it is worth looking to see which illustrations you prefer and suit your work best)
Soffel, J., (2016) 'What are the 21-first century skills every student needs?' *World Economic Forum*: https://www.weforum.org/agenda/2016/03/21st-century-skills-future-jobs-students/

For more ideas and information you can also visit Helen Porter's website: www.outsidelearning.co.uk

Index

adaptation and evolution 53
algebra 120
Ancient Greek games 77
angles 119
animals
  circulatory system 32
  digestive system 30
  food chains 31
  healthy lifestyle 33
  human body labelling 27
  human skeletons 29
  identification 26
  investigation of 34
  needs of 28
  water and nutrients requirement 34
art and design outdoors 100
  inspirations 105–6
  outside materials 101–5

Baghdad, creation of 81
Bedouin tents building 81
brain function, and physical activity 4
bridges, building 67

calculations 116–17
cave painting 62
Celtic/Viking village creation 72
cityscapes 104–5
cleaning dirty water 92
compass use 96, 97
country quiz 84–5
creative writing 110

dirty water, cleaning 92

earth and space study
  investigations of 53
  solar system 52
English outdoors 107–8
  grammar 112–11
  reading 108–10
  spelling 112
  writing 110–12
environmental art 101–2
environmental changes 45
evolution and inheritance study 53

fact finding 56
field sketch 89
flints sorting 60
flood plains investigation 73
flowering plants, structure of common 19–25
food chains and food sources 43
Forest School approach 11
fossils 39, 61

geography outdoors 83
  compass use 96, 97
  country quiz 84–5
  geographical skills and fieldwork 96–9
  human and physical geography 90–5
  locational knowledge 83–4
  map drawing 86
  place knowledge 87–90
  standardised symbols 98–9
geometry
  angles 119
  2D and 3D shapes 118

habitats 41, 42
history outdoors 54
    Ancient Greek games 77
    Baghdad, creation of 81
    Bedouin tents, building 81
    bridges, building 67
    cave painting 62
    Celtic/Viking village creation 72
    flints sorting 60
    flood plains investigation 73
    fossils study 61
    herbal tea making 71
    Islamic patterns 80
    living memory, beyond 58
    living memory, changes with 57
    mazes, drawing 79
    natural dyes making 68
    Neolithic stone balls 63
    Nine Men's Morris game 68
    Olympic Games 77
    paper making 75
    Roman marching 66
    Roman mosaic patterns 65
    Roman mosaic pictures 64
    shadufs making 73
    wattle and daub 70
human and physical geography
    cleaning dirty water 92
    geographical vocabulary 90
    land use 95
    rivers 90
    volcanoes 93
    water cycle 94

Islamic patterns 80

land art 101–2
landscapes 104–5
land use 95
life cycle, of plants 24–5
light
    investigation of 50
    and shadow 48
    travel of 49
living plants 21
living things
    classification of 44, 47
    and environmental changes 45
    food chains and food sources 43

habitats 41, 42
    identification of 44
    investigation of 48
    life cycles 46
    micro-habitats 41
    reproductive system 46
local area investigations 88

map drawing 86
map investigations 87
materials
    everyday materials 36
    investigation of 36
    objects and materials investigation 35
maths outdoors 114
    algebra 120
    calculations 116–17
    fractions 117
    geometry 118–19
    measurement 117–18
    numbers 115–16
    ratio and proportions 120
    statistics 119
matter, state of 37
measurement
    length, area and perimeter 117–18
    money 118
micro-habitats 41

National Curriculum
    art and design 100
    English 107–8
    geography 83
    history 54
    maths 114
    science 16–17
natural dye making 68
Neolithic stone balls 63
Nine Men's Morris game 68
non-fiction writing 111–12
numbers
    counting 115
    times tables 115–16

observational drawing and painting 103–4
outdoor learning 10–15
    benefits of 2–3, 11, 12
    day to day experiences 12
    definition of 13

early days of planning 11–12
idea of 10–11
rationale for 1–3
settings for 10
whole- school approach 10

paper making 75
physical activity, and brain function 4
place knowledge 90
    field sketch 89
    local area investigations 88
    maps investigations 87
plants
    description of 22
    identification 18
    investigation of 25
    life cycle 24–5
    living plants 21
    observation of 20
    structure of common flowering plants
        19–25
    variation in 23
playground art 105–6
poetry 111

ratios 120
reading 108
    inference and deduction 109
    story walks and story lines 109–10
    understanding and engagement 109
reproductive system 46
resourcing 6
rivers 90
rocks
    fossils 39
    learning about 38
Roman marching 66
Roman mosaic patterns 65
Roman mosaic pictures 64

safety 7–8
science outdoors
    animals 26–34
    earth and space 52–3
    evolution and inheritance 53
    fossils 39

light 48–50
living things 41–8
materials 35–6
plants 18–25
rocks 38
seasons observation 40
sound 50–1
state of matter 34
water cycle 37
seasons observation 40
shadow 48
shadufs making 73
solar system 52
sound
    investigations of 51
    volume of 50–1
spelling 112
standardised symbols 98–9
statistics
    bar graphs 119
    Carroll diagram 119
    Venn diagram 119
story stones 110–11
story walks and story lines 109–10

3D work 102–3
timelines 55
times tables 115
    cards 115
    hopscotch 115
    run and find 116
2D and 3D shapes 118

Venn diagram 119
vocabulary and paragraphs 113
volcanoes 93

water cycle 37, 94
wattle and daub 70
weather conditions 8
whole-school approach 10
writing
    creative writing 110
    non-fiction writing 111–12
    poetry 111
    story stones 110–11